NO · WASTE
SAVE · THE · PLANET
VEGAN
COOKBOOK

NO·WASTE
SAVE·THE·PLANET
VEGAN
COOKBOOK

100 Plant-Based Recipes and
100 Kitchen-Tested Tips
for Waste-Free Meatless Cooking

CELINE STEEN

HARVARD
COMMON
PRESS

Brimming with creative inspiration, how-to projects, and useful information to enrich your everyday life, Quarto Knows is a favorite destination for those pursuing their interests and passions. Visit our site and dig deeper with our books into your area of interest: Quarto Creates, Quarto Cooks, Quarto Homes, Quarto Lives, Quarto Drives, Quarto Explores, Quarto Gifts, or Quarto Kids.

First Published in 2021 by The Harvard Common Press, an imprint of The Quarto Group, 100 Cummings Center, Suite 265-D, Beverly, MA 01915, USA.
T (978) 282-9590 F (978) 283-2742 QuartoKnows.com

The Harvard Common Press titles are also available at discount for retail, wholesale, promotional, and bulk purchase. For details, contact the Special Sales Manager by email at specialsales@quarto.com or by mail at The Quarto Group, Attn: Special Sales Manager, 100 Cummings Center, Suite 265-D, Beverly, MA 01915, USA.

Library of Congress Cataloging-in-Publication Data

Names: Steen, Celine, author.
Title: No-waste save-the-planet vegan cookbook : 100 plant-based recipes
   and 100 kitchen-tested tips for waste-free meatless cooking / Celine
   Steen.
Description: Beverly, MA : Harvard Common Press, 2021. | Includes index.
Identifiers: LCCN 2021004702 (print) | LCCN 2021004703 (ebook) | ISBN
   9781592339914 (hardback) | ISBN 9781631599798 (ebook)
Subjects: LCSH: Vegan cooking. | Food waste. | LCGFT: Cookbooks.
Classification: LCC TX837 .S7365 2021 (print) | LCC TX837 (ebook) | DDC
   641.5/6362--dc23
LC record available at https://lccn.loc.gov/2021004702
LC ebook record available at https://lccn.loc.gov/2021004703

Design and Page Layout: Samantha J. Bednarek, samanthabednarek.com

Printed in China

25 24 23 22 21   1 2 3 4 5

ISBN: 978-1-59233-991-4

Digital edition published in 2021
eISBN: 978-1-63159-979-8

DEDICATION

This book was written in memory of my beloved mom, Monique Narbel-Gimzia. Putting into words how your absence has impacted me is an impossible task. I see you in every bird and every shooting star. *Je t'aime de tout mon coeur pour toujours, ma Mamounette Noisette.*

CONTENTS

PREFACE
10

CHAPTER 1
THE VEGAN
NO•WASTE KITCHEN
15

CHAPTER 2
BREAKFAST
27

Mandarin-White Chocolate Scones 28
Coconut Carrot Cookies 29
Cocoa Nut Hummus 30
Chunky Nut Granola 31
Breakfast Rice Pudding 32
Soured-Oat Hand Waffles 34
Breakfast Greeña Colada 35
Pink Latte 37
Pineapple Berry Swirl Smoothie 38
Baked Sweet Potato Bread 39
Plain Jane Sourdough Waffles 40
The Whole Lemon Curd 41
Lemon Curd Muffins 42
AB & Fermented J Pots de Crème 43
Overnight Granola Bowl 44
Banana Berry Smoothie Bowl 45
Trail Mix Cookies 46
Halva Scones 47
Beer Nut Granola 48
Salty Beer Caramel Sauce 50
Miso Caramel Spread 51

The Whole Banana-nola Bread 52
Baked Banana Nut Oatmeal 53
Congee Bowl 55
Flax Crackers 57
Barbecue Chickpea Scramble 58

CHAPTER 3
MAIN COURSES
61

Chaat Masala Peas and Quinoa Stew 62
Chaat Masala Chickpea Pockets 63
Pineapple Tamarind Chutney 64
Sriracha Barbecue Sauce 65
Herby Quinoa Frittata 66
Yuzu Koji Tempeh Sandwiches 67
Mamou's Favorite Miso Bowls 68
Smoky Sausages 70
Pulled Jackfruit Sandwiches 71
Moroccan Quinoa Veggie Bowl 73
Zippy Herb Dressing 75
Sichuan-Flavored Mushrooms with Roasted
   Shishito Peppers 77
Sweet and Sour Carrot Tarte Tatin 78
Spicy Bean Burgers 81
Chili Mac Gratin 82
Pistachio Dukkah Whole Cauliflower 83
My Favorite Bowl of Veggies 84
Savory Sweet Cluck-Free Strips Sandwiches 87
Kimchi Fried "Noodz" 88
Sloppy Bulgogi 89
Smoky Sriracha Tacos 90
Pineapple Fried Rice 93
Muhammara 94
Cashew Sour Cream and Lasagna Sauce 95
Butternut Squash Lasagna 96
Aquafaba Ranch Dressing 98
Ropa Vieja Tacos 99

Pink Latte
page 37

Tomato Hummus Soup
page 154

CHAPTER 4
SIDES

101

Creton **102**
Creton en Croûte **103**
Smoky Carrot Spread **104**
Noochy Sourdough Crackers **107**
Olive Fennel Hummus **108**
Basil–Carrot Top Pesto **109**
Orange-Habanero Jam **110**
Orange-Habanero Corn Bread **112**
Red Curry Peanut Sauce **113**
Pickled Turmeric Carrots **114**
Pickled Red Onions **115**
Fennel Kimchi **117**
Queso'rprise **118**
Umami Sofrito **119**
Go-to Nut Butter Dressing **120**
Miso Sake Sauce **121**
Roasted Potato Beer Salad **122**
Spicy Glazed Root Veggies **124**
Za'atar Chutney **125**
Beet Crumble **126**
Labneh **127**
Potato Roesti **128**
Savory Pickle Waffles **129**
Sour Cream Onion Scones **131**
Pomegranate Ezme **132**
Smoky Carrot Meatless Balls **133**

CHAPTER 5
SOUPS AND STEWS

135

Finishing Brown Sauce **136**
Everything but the Kitchen Sink
    Leftover Veggies Stew **138**
Kimchi-ckpea Stew **139**
Roasted Onion Soup **141**
A Guide to Veggie Broth **142**
Uncanny Chickpeas **145**
Baba Ghanoush Soup **146**
Sunset Stew **147**
Root Veggie Gumbo **148**
Mushroom Corn Chip Chili **150**
Carrot Top–Pea Soup with Pesto **153**
Tomato Hummus Soup **154**

CHAPTER 6
DESSERTS AND SNACKS

157

Citrus Quark-alike Cake **158**
Coconut Pudding **159**
"Compost" Cookies **160**
Moroccan Cranachan **162**
Sheet Pan Apple Crisp **164**
Beer Nut Shortbread **165**
Chocolate Banana Peanut Pie **166**
Peanut-Fudge Brownies **167**
Peanut-Chocolate Fudge **168**
Any Fruit Frangipane Galette **169**
Fudgy Sesame Chocolate Mug Cake **172**

Acknowledgments **175**
Purveyors **176**
About the Author **177**
Index **178**

PREFACE

My sweet mom passed away rather suddenly a couple of months before I embarked on this new cookbook project.

Well, it sure is a sobering way to begin this book. What does it have to do with anything? Oh, it has *everything* to do with it. She was my best friend. She was also a big part of my cookbook writing process—from sharing the excitement of a new contract, to coming up with ideas for fun recipes, to testing every single one of them, provided she could gather all the ingredients back home in Switzerland. That's every single recipe from every cookbook I ever wrote. That's a lot.

Not to digress from the subject matter at hand here. The reason I am sharing this with you, patient reader, is that she was adamant about not wasting anything, taking care to properly recycle every single piece of plastic and paper. Those veggie scraps she just couldn't do anything with? Off to the compost bin they went. The Swiss aren't kidding about their dedication to recycling properly!

So, when the offer presented itself to write a no-waste cookbook, even though my grief was (and still is) extremely painful and raw, I simply couldn't pass it up. In her honor mostly, but also because it's something I'm increasingly passionate about.

I started writing most of this preface before the Covid-19 pandemic took place. And then it happened, with folks worldwide having to self-isolate at home for more than a month . . . and counting, at the time of writing. Limiting trips outdoors was also highly encouraged: so, grocery shopping shrank to the bare minimum, and most farmers' markets closed temporarily for business. Although I cannot foretell the future and don't know the outcome of this global event, I know that during it, people have become more creative than ever in their ways of cooking, to avoid wasting the more limited goods they have available. Financial hardship also hit many of us due to loss of employment and so we've become more aware of the value of the groceries we buy with our hard-earned money. The vegetables or bread you allowed to become limp and moldy just a few months before, throwing them away without blinking? There's no way we let that happen now. With a stricter shopping list and more clever storage ideas, let's turn at least one aspect of the pandemic into a positive: less food waste. So, not only does this book share ways to use all the parts of many fruits and vegetables, but it also offers creative solutions to use that jar of Vegemite hidden in the dark corners of your cupboard, those fermented black soybeans you used once then promptly forgot about, and more.

Mamou's Favorite
Miso Bowls
page 68

Pistachio Dukkah
Whole Cauliflower
page 83

As most of us are aware, in this day and age, planet Earth needs to catch a break from the innumerable ways we humans have caused her harm. Look at the weekly (if not daily) amount of trash create, no matter your household size: now, multiply this by the 7.8 billion folks who inhabit this place (as of the time of writing). How's that for depressing? We like to fool ourselves into thinking that recycling performs miracles and solves most issues, but all it takes is watching documentaries on the subject to realize it isn't quite so simple. The outlook is bleak if we don't put our helmets on and finally go to war on waste.

I recommend the films *Broken*, *Trashed*, and *Plastic Paradise* for more background on the planetary costs of both the quantity of waste and the dangerous materials in household waste.

I can faintly hear the voices of a few people pondering if being vegan isn't already a good enough commitment to try to make Earth a better place. That is speaking environmentally and, of course, for the animals. Granted, it is a big step toward improvement, but the reality is that the vegan lifestyle doesn't necessarily equate with a complete no-waste lifestyle. Just like it is possible to be vegan and eat unhealthy foods, it is also entirely possible to eat vegan and throw far more foods and goods into the trash than seems reasonable.

Before I get started with statistics and other snooze-inducing numbers in the next chapter, it is important to remind ourselves that perfection is not the goal. Just as it may take time and some failed attempts for newbie vegans to fully commit to the lifestyle, we're not looking for every little scrap of waste to be saved from the trash or compost.

Making efforts, trying to improve on the current status, and getting rid of habits that aren't good for anyone are the ultimate goals. Imagine if everyone did their small part to make the world a better place, instead of thinking, *I am but a drop in the ocean of folks who just can't be bothered*. A drop plus a drop and another drop can lead to a full ocean of positive change, provided enough people become involved in the movement.

It's a relief to see an increasing number of businesses, smaller and larger, joining in the effort to reduce waste by offering reusable straws, bags, and more. Some coffee shops even encourage you to bring your own cup to be filled with your beverage of choice. They will also, oftentimes, give you a discount for simply doing that. How's that for awesome? (Of course, that cannot take place during the aforementioned pandemic.)

One has to wonder when and how we all started becoming at peace with tossing foods that we don't finish, or throwing away goods that don't look perfectly photogenic. It seems that previous generations were far more conservative and respectful in their approach to leftovers and didn't blink twice when it came to cooking with bruised produce.

This cookbook is an attempt to get us back to that mindset, offering tips with every recipe that will, hopefully, help you on your journey to reducing waste, and making good use of everything that populates your cupboards, refrigerator, and maybe even garden if you're lucky enough to have one! We can do this, everyone.

CHAPTER 1

THE VEGAN NO·WASTE KITCHEN

On average, Americans toss 4½ pounds (2 kg) of garbage every day. Multiply that by about 7.8 billion (the number of people living on Earth at the time of writing) and you get a painful reminder of why right now is the time to do our part to reduce waste.

Clearly, I do not know what your path toward cracking open this cookbook was. Are you a seasoned vegan looking for ways to make the most of your food purchases? Or, are you new both to veganism and to lower food waste? So many possibilities, so little time.

WHY VEGAN AND NO WASTE?

Veganism isn't solely for the sake of animals, although it is the most important reason to many of us vegans. Adding more plant-based meals into one's diet has environmental benefits as well. That's because the production of plant-based ingredients usually involves lower emissions of greenhouse gas than diets that include animal products. Raising livestock means having to feed it, making use of more resources that could go toward feeding more humans in the first place. That's why, overall, producing meat has a greater negative impact on the environment than a plant-based diet does.

 To learn more about how plant-based diets are friendlier to the planet than meat-based diets, watch the films *Cowspiracy*, *Forks over Knives*, and *More than Honey*.

About 50 percent of all produce purchased in the United States ends up in the trash, then in landfills. Because produce is a rather affordable commodity here, we purchase more than we can eat, only to see it spoil before we can get around to cooking it. You'd think that since produce comes with its own natural packaging (think: orange and banana peels), it wouldn't be a problem, as it should quickly biodegrade, right? Sadly, wrong. Landfills are too overpacked to allow oxygen to circulate, and biodegradation needs oxygen to occur. That's where composting comes into play.

There are two ways to bring composting into your life: through commercial composting, via your city's waste management, if that's a service they offer (though possibly at a cost), or farmers' markets, some of which offer composting options, too. The best way to find out what's available in your area is to perform an online search. You will also be able to find out which items are acceptable for composting, as it varies by location. It is fairly safe to assume that straightforward plant-based items, such as fruit and vegetable matters, as well as grass clippings, should be accepted.

In the meantime, whether it be through pickups or taking your commercial composting to a specific location, you will need a compost bin to store the goods until it's time to part with them. Any airtight container will do, ideally with a charcoal filter in the lid to prevent odors and keep bugs away, especially in warm conditions.

The alternative to commercial composting is to make your own compost, whether it is in your backyard if you have one, or simply in your kitchen. So, how do you begin? Find a dedicated spot in your yard for your compost pile, preferably in the shade and away from moisture.

A Guide to
Veggie Broth
page 142

How do you build a healthy compost pile? By combining equal parts green matter (vegetable food scraps, grass, etc.), with brown matter (dirt, twigs, leaves, etc.), water (through periodical watering with a hose, to dampness but not soakage), and, last but not least, air (through periodical stirring with a pitchfork or shovel). All this will help the compost break down over time. Chop larger pieces of green or brown matter into smaller sizes to help accelerate the process. With so many variables, it's hard to give an accurate estimate of how long this breakdown will take. It could be anywhere between a couple of weeks or months to, sometimes, even years!

If you're going to compost indoors, invest in a compost bin fitted with a charcoal filter that will need occasional replacement (normally every two months, but this lifespan could vary by brand). I like to have two separate compost bins in the kitchen. That's because I throw spent coffee grounds onto the mulch that adorns our front yard. I actually don't use it to fertilize the soil or plants, but to prevent cats and dogs from using it as a litter box. Whatever works, right? Begone, kitties and pups (but, really, I do love you).

Note that coffee grounds should not be used to fertilize every plant out there. Plants that like highly acidic soil will thrive with this addition. Others will react poorly to it, such as aloe vera, radish, watercress, and more. Be sure to research this before "grounding" your plant.

Hate the mess composting may leave behind in your bins? Look for biodegradable liners to keep things a bit cleaner. When full, just toss the bag, along with the composting contents, and it degrades in an environmentally friendly manner, too.

Although it is good to have composting options to help reduce our footprint in landfills, the most surefire way to avoid food waste is to avoid purchasing too much food in the first place. Easier said than done in pandemic times, where trips to the grocery store should be kept to a strict minimum. In more normal times, however, it is best to purchase perishable items as needed so they don't get a chance to spoil. The fewer items one stores in cupboards, refrigerator, and freezer, the easier it is to keep track of what's there.

If, despite your best attempt at keeping yourself in check as far as food purchases go, you still find yourself with more produce than you can handle, don't be afraid to enlist your freezer to help. Most fresh fruits and vegetables will freeze beautifully for future use. Canning is also a great option, as is using a food dehydrator for long-term storage. Donating the extra food to neighbors, friends, family, or food banks, can be a welcome alternative. Check with food banks in your area about the type of donations they accept before them bringing anything because their policies can vary.

I love to dedicate a whole weekend morning or afternoon to meal prepping for the week ahead. The oven will be hot anyway, pans of vegetables can roast at the same time, and some pots don't even need to be cleaned between batches of different foods. Sure, it can be a lot of work for a single morning, but it ensures foods are being used at their peak freshness and reduces overall time in the kitchen during the week. Consider enlisting family members to help with the cooking and cleanup: it's a great way to connect, have a chat, and to share fun memories.

Just as your first steps as a new vegan made you want to get rid of all the non-vegan items in your possession (that leather wallet you've had for ages, those soaps that have probably been tested on animals), you might feel the urge to get rid of the non-environmentally friendly goods that populate your kitchen and bathroom. I'm talking about that roll of cling paper silently mocking you every time you use it or the aluminum foil hugging your sandwiches, not to mention those plastic toothbrushes having a party in your mouth. It's a respectable and understandable feeling, but unless you donate it all to someone who will put it to good use, it is a waste in and of itself. Why not finish what you have, then make sure to purchase Earth-friendly items going forward?

GETTING STARTED IN YOUR VEGAN NO–WASTE KITCHEN

One of the main messages I want you to take away from this cookbook is to use recipes only as guidelines. Not everyone likes the same levels of spice or has the chance to include gluten or soy in their diet, and so many people don't care for Brussels sprouts the way I do. So, tweak carefully, but most importantly, have fun being creative and making changes.

Each recipe comes "equipped" with a little no waste–related tip to help you on your way to wasting less food, water, and energy—be it in the kitchen, garden, or anywhere.

soy-free

gluten-free

fast-forward

Recipes are marked with icons to highlight those that have the potential to be free of soy (**SF**, as in soy-free, provided all ingredients used are certified soy-free); free of gluten (**GF**, as in gluten-free, provided all ingredients used are certified gluten-free), and, finally, those that take less than 30 minutes of preparation and cooking time together (**FF**, as in fast-forward).

INGREDIENTS

Here is a list of a few frequently used ingredients in this book that might call for a little more explanation. Anything more obscure than this is addressed directly in the recipe.

FEELING SALTY?

I love using kosher salt because it's harder to overdo it when adding it by the pinch, as it is less potent than regular salt. I use the Diamond brand, which is also less salty than the Morton brand of kosher salt. Why? Because of the shape the grains of kosher salt are pressed into. Morton kosher salt grains are flat, whereas Diamond kosher salt grains are pyramid shaped. You'd think at least salt would be simple, but that would be a hard no. Let's try to make life just a little easier with the following rule of thumb regarding the salt you can get your pinch-y fingers on:

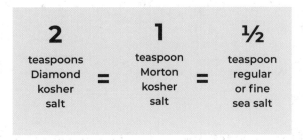

Or, 2:1:½. Got it? Good.

MISO

I use white (shiro) miso. It is milder and slightly sweeter than misos that are fermented for a longer period, and so it is more versatile as it can be used in both savory and sweet applications. If you eat a lot of miso, or are a fan of bolder umami-rich flavors, I recommend stocking red miso as well. Regardless of the kind of miso you choose, storing it in the refrigerator in an airtight container is the most surefire way to keep it for as long as possible, which is about a year, before the flavor might start becoming less favorable.

NUTRITIONAL YEAST

This ingredient isn't quite as obscure as it once was. Even sites-slash-magazines like *Bon Appétit* make use of it in their most popular recipes—vegan or not. With lots of umami packed in this inactive yeast product, you can make your dishes a little cheesier and more flavorful. Because things are usually just a touch more complicated than they should be, be aware that nutritional yeast is sold in flake form as well as a powder. I use the finer powder, which, of course, weighs more than the flakes when measured in a tablespoon (or cup, if you like the "nooch" a lot.) So, keep the following in mind:

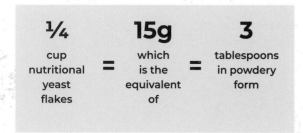

¼ cup nutritional yeast flakes = 15g which is the equivalent of = 3 tablespoons in powdery form

You can always give a few pulses to the flakes in your food processor if you want the finer kind, which makes for better broths and smoother results overall, in my humble opinion.

ROASTED NUT AND SEED OILS

I use these, on occasion, in my recipes. I buy bottles of the stuff only when I can get a good deal. They can be a bit costly when no good discounts are to be found, so feel free to replace them with whatever oil you have on hand. Regular olive oil (not extra-virgin) or grapeseed oil are my go-tos as far as neutral-flavored oils. If available and affordable, though, roasted oils are a great way to add a fantastic flavor boost to your dishes.

A FEW GOOD TOOLS

As long as you have a stove, an oven, a handful of bowls, plates, spatulas, pans, and lots of enthusiasm, you should be set to make most of the recipes in this book. But a few of the following special items do come in handy on occasion and make your cooking life just a touch more easy-going.

FERMENTATION CROCK

If you're a kimchi aficionado or would love to make your own sauerkraut, I recommend investing in a crock solely dedicated to fermentation. Sure, glass jars work in a pinch, but I find crocks to be more reliable and yield better results on the flavor front. I got mine with a water lock aimed to keep bugs at bay and water weights to keep the vegetables immersed in the brine.

KITCHEN SCALE

You might have noticed that this cookbook lists both weights and cup (volumes) measurements. That's been the case for all the books I've written, and over the years, I have become a big proponent of weighing ingredients. It's just more accurate and, oftentimes, even simpler to do as it calls for fewer tablespoons and cups to clean up. I use a twenty-buck Escali-brand kitchen scale that's quite efficient and long-lasting, too: mine is more than ten years old and is used on a daily basis, yet the batteries rarely need to be changed.

SALAD SPINNER

Yes, the most obvious use for this tool is to spin-dry fragile greens to maximize their lifespan. But don't limit yourself to salads! Absolutely any herb, vegetable (even cubed potatoes), or legume (chickpeas before sautéing) can be spun-dry in this nifty tool. Removing moisture allows for better caramelization whenever roasting or sautéing. Think of it this way: any food that has excess moisture will steam rather than caramelize. And where does flavor lie? In caramelization! So, spin it right round, baby, right round.

COMPOST BIN

I like to use a transitional bin to bring vegetable scraps and coffee grounds directly to the main composting area. You can use anything really, as long as it's airtight and large enough to handle a fair amount of scraps—but not so large it takes over your whole kitchen counter. Favor those with a charcoal filter to prevent odors. These usually last about two months. I purchased two of the bins made by Bamboozle. They get mitigated reviews, but I have no complaints so far.

HIGH-SPEED BLENDER

Although I'm quite reluctant to include this tool as it can be cost-prohibitive, I cannot help but sing the praises of this machine. I hesitated for years before finally taking the plunge. This tool has made a world of difference in the textures of my soups, dips, sauces, smoothies—and it even saved my marriage! Okay, kidding about that last one. But it is a worthwhile investment if you can afford the expense and the counter space it takes. Birthday present, perhaps? For the next twenty years? That was my trick for justifying it. I have a Vitamix, but I hear good things about Ninja and Blendtec brands as well.

MINI FOOD PROCESSOR OR BLENDER

I know, you only have so much counter space and I keep throwing more equipment your way. But hear me out: these mini machines are so fantastic when it comes to whipping up a quick dressing, or spread, or even just to chop a whole lemon or orange, peel and all! They aren't necessarily costly: I use the Ninja Express Chop, and it cost me less than $20. It's quite sturdy and efficient, not to mention far easier to clean than a larger machine. I've used mine for more than three years now without issue.

SILICONE SPATULAS

These are lifesavers. Super sturdy, lightweight, and heat resistant, they can be used for everything. Cooking, prep, serving, you name it. Wooden spoons have undeniable charm, too, but silicone spatulas are slowly taking over for their job in the kitchen. They are far easier to care for, as they don't need frequent application of mineral oil like wooden spoons do. My favorite brand is GIR (Get It Right): they offer a wide array of shapes and colors and the price point is fair. Did I mention they offer a lifetime guarantee?

VEGETABLE AND FRUIT BRUSH

If you're going to use the peel of your potatoes, carrots, oranges, and bananas, you want to make sure they are scrubbed super clean. These little brushes are affordable and do a perfect job. Make sure to give them a good cleaning after each use and let them air-dry thoroughly so they don't get moldy.

THE SHELF LIFESPAN OF FOOD

You know how the internet comes with that one rule everyone should follow but never does? Don't read the comments. Right. So, in the food world, there should be one that says. "Don't trust the best-by dates." These dates are more of a guideline regarding freshness and quality, but not a sign the food is to be tossed because it is suddenly inedible or a food-safety issue. It isn't like your nut milk is going to—POOF!—go sour on you when April 15 comes along. And your bread will not break into moldy mayhem when the date printed on its packaging is upon us. You can trust your nose, first and foremost, and your eyes, too.

As far as storing food goes, I live in an area where it gets really hot in summer and humidity is pretty high in our house. These facts make it so that I'm better off putting all my food in the refrigerator if I want it to last for more than a few days. But if you live in a fairly temperate climate area and don't see your bread go moldy after just one day on the counter, you can be a little more lenient when it comes to storing produce and other goods.

A FEW RULES OF THUMB:

1 Remove (and recycle) any potential packaging before storing fruits and vegetables. Don't store fruit and vegetables together. Fruit (apples for example) release gases that will spoil vegetables faster. Also, always separate onions and potatoes, as the former will accelerate spud sprouting on the latter.

2 You can, and should, always store citrus fruit, tomatoes, onions, potatoes, and garlic at room temperature for best flavor and texture.

3 On the other hand, any produce that has been chopped or peeled should be refrigerated. Mushrooms, cucumbers, zucchini, delicate herbs such as basil, chives, cilantro, or parsley, or anything that is soft and a wee bit fragile, should be refrigerated for longer life. It's best to gently dry whatever's been exposed to excessive moisture before a trip to the refrigerator. For example, local grocery stores spray their refrigerated produce to make it look more appealing and fresh, but what it really does is cause premature spoilage. I really wish they would cut it out, but short of throwing a fit in the produce aisle (cleanup in aisle 9!), I simply pat the goods dry before storing them in the refrigerator's vegetable drawer.

4 Oils such as grapeseed oil or extra-virgin olive oil should be stored away from direct light to preserve freshness. Nuts and seeds, as well as oils made from nuts and seeds, should be stored in the refrigerator to keep them from going rancid.

5 Grains and flours should be stored in the refrigerator or freezer to keep them fresh, but also to prevent insects from having a field day with them. At the very least, those food items should be stored in an airtight, preferably glass, container if kept at room temperature. I've seen some bugs be quite determined to find a way in and it is so exhausting to get rid of them once they are in. (I'm looking at you, weevils.)

CHAPTER 2

BREAKFAST

Are you awake yet? Good! Then you can put your no-waste resolutions to the test even before holding a steaming cup of whatever hot beverage you like in your hand! Lesson number one: do not toss coffee grounds or teabags in the trash once they're respectively brewed or steeped. They can be recycled to prevent overcrowding the trash and making nuisances of themselves in overcrowded landfills.

MANDARIN—WHITE CHOCOLATE SCONES

FF These little bundles of morning happiness are so fragrant it will be hard not to devour them straight from the oven. Go for it, if that's your thing! I prefer mine slightly cooled down, but you do you. And you deserve chocolate for breakfast. Hey, there's a whole mandarin in the goods. Surely that means it's good for you? Should you have trouble locating vegan white chocolate chips, no one will be mad if you go for semisweet chocolate instead.

1¼ cups (150 g) all-purpose flour

¼ cup (30 g) sliced almonds

⅓ cup (70 g) packed light brown sugar (weighed to make sure)

1½ teaspoons baking powder

½ teaspoon Diamond kosher salt

1 medium-size mandarin, skin on, scrubbed clean and patted dry, chopped

¼ cup (56 g) cold coconut oil

Plant-based milk, as needed (I use 3 tablespoons, or 45 ml)

Generous ½ cup (100 g) vegan white chocolate chips

1. Preheat the oven to 375°F (190°C, or gas mark 5). Line a baking sheet with a silicone baking mat or a piece of parchment paper.

2. In a food processor, combine the flour, almonds, brown sugar, baking powder, and salt. Process until the almonds are ground. Add the mandarin and coconut oil. Pulse about 10 times to combine.

3. Add the milk, 1 tablespoon (15 ml) at a time, pulsing just until a dough forms: the dough should hold together easily without being too dry or too wet. Fold and press the chocolate chips into the dough. Shape the dough into a 6-inch (15 cm) disk and divide it into 6 equal triangles. Flatten the triangles just slightly to reshape and place on the prepared sheet, leaving at least 1 inch (2.5 cm) between each scone.

4. Bake for 14 to 16 minutes, or until golden brown. Let cool slightly before enjoying.

5. Leftovers can be wrapped tightly and stored at room temperature for up to 1 day. Reheat in a 325°F (170°C, or gas mark 3) oven for 8 to 10 minutes to revive.

Yield: 6 scones

PLANET SAVER TIP 1

Who knew you could throw the whole fruit in your baked goods? Well, not all of them (don't try this with a pineapple), but it does work for quite a few. Purchase organic fruit and remove all labels or other unwanted man-made additions. Scrub the fruit with a soft fruit brush and pat dry before use.

COCONUT CARROT COOKIES

Yes, I do enjoy the occasional cookie for breakfast. Sometimes a little treat is the only thing that will make the day easier to deal with. You know the feeling, too, I'm sure. If you don't want to bake the cookies as soon as the dough is ready, or if you want to enjoy these warm and bake as needed, refrigerate the dough in an airtight container for up to 1 week, and shape it when cookie time arrives while the oven preheats.

1 cup (110 g) minced carrot (can use unpeeled, keep the tops for other recipes)

3 tablespoons (20 g) toasted coconut flakes

¼ cup (60 ml) roasted peanut oil or other oil

¼ cup (56 g) unrefined coconut oil, melted

¼ cup (60 g) plain or vanilla plant-based yogurt

¾ cup (weight varies, about 150 g) granulated sweetener of choice (cane sugar, coconut sugar, Sucanat, etc.)

2 tablespoons (40 g) blackstrap molasses

1 cup plus 2 tablespoons (135 g) whole-wheat flour

1 cup (80 g) quick cooking oats

½ cup (75 g) raisins

1 teaspoon baking powder

1 teaspoon ground cinnamon

½ teaspoon Diamond kosher salt

⅛ teaspoon grated nutmeg

1. Preheat the oven to 350°F (180°C, or gas mark 4). Line a baking sheet with a silicone baking mat.

2. In a small food processor, pulse the carrot and coconut a few times until coarsely ground. Transfer to a large bowl and stir in the oils, yogurt, sweetener, and molasses.

3. Add the flour, oats, raisins, baking powder, cinnamon, salt, and nutmeg. Use a spatula to combine the ingredients thoroughly. Use ¼ cup (75 g) packed dough to shape each cookie. Place the cookies on the prepared baking sheet about 1 inch (2.5 cm) apart and flatten slightly, as they won't spread much while baking.

4. Bake for about 22 minutes until golden brown and fragrant. Transfer the sheet to a cooling rack and let cool before enjoying. I love these chilled from the fridge—they get extra chewy.

5. Refrigerate leftovers in an airtight container for up to 3 days.

Yield: 10 big cookies

PLANET SAVER TIP 2

Don't have yogurt? Use applesauce, or even a flax egg! Combine 1 tablespoon (7 g) ground flaxseed with 3 tablespoons (45 ml) water. Let stand 5 minutes. Don't like raisins? Use dates or toasted walnuts. Gotta love recipes that allow substitutions.

COCOA NUT HUMMUS

   I love to serve this sweet hummus on bread, with waffles, or even to dip pretzels into for a slightly healthier snack. After all, chickpeas are loaded with fiber and protein. And those are healthy things to have. Use whichever nut butter you prefer. Hazelnut would be nice, paired with hazelnut oil, too. My go-to is roasted peanut butter with roasted peanut oil, because those two are less expensive alternatives and I'm a bit of a tightwad, I suppose.

1⅓ cups (227 g) cooked chickpeas

⅓ cup (86 g) roasted nut butter of choice

¼ cup (60 ml) roasted nut oil of choice or (56 g) coconut oil

¼ cup (80 g) liquid sweetener of choice, or to taste

⅓ cup (25 g) unsweetened cocoa powder

Diamond kosher salt, to taste

1 teaspoon pure vanilla extract

1. In a food processor, combine all the ingredients and process until mostly smooth. Taste and add more sweetener to taste.

2. Refrigerate in an airtight container for up to 1 week. If using coconut oil, the spread will harden more than with a roasted nut oil. Bring to room temperature for about 15 minutes before serving to spread more easily.

Yield: 1 pound (454 g)

PLANET SAVER TIP 3

Ever since I became frustrated with a certain brand that sold cans of chickpeas containing the wrong amount of beans per can (lots of liquid, not enough beans), I started cooking my own—with far better results. My point is, it might take a little more time than just grabbing a can opener, but it saves a lot of money and waste. Something important to keep in mind when making this recipe: use chickpeas that weren't cooked with ingredients such as garlic or herbs, otherwise your sweet hummus will be all kinds of wrong.

CHUNKY NUT GRANOLA

Not a fan of peanuts? Switch things up using a different nut butter, or even seed butter. If you like your granola with extra add-ins, such as raisins, chocolate chips, dried cherries, or what-have-you, add them once the granola has cooled. I like to serve my granola on top of yogurt with a spoonful of strawberry jam for some PB&J action.

½ cup (160 g) agave nectar

¼ cup (36 g) coconut sugar or (48 g) Sucanat

¾ cup plus 2 tablespoons (224 g) crunchy peanut butter

2 tablespoons (10 g) unsweetened cocoa powder

¼ cup (60 ml) roasted peanut oil or other oil

½ teaspoon Diamond kosher salt

2 cups (160 g) old-fashioned rolled oats

1 cup (115 g) whole-grain nuggets (such as Grape-Nuts) or any sturdy, lightly sweetened breakfast cereal (such as Cheerios)

½ cup (84 g) whole golden flaxseed, ground

1. Preheat the oven to 300°F (150°C, or gas mark 2). Line two large rimmed baking sheets with silicone baking mats.

2. In a large bowl, stir together the agave, coconut sugar, peanut butter, cocoa powder, oil, and salt to combine thoroughly.

3. Add the oats, nuggets, and flaxseed. Stir to coat thoroughly. Divide the mixture among the prepared sheets, making sure to flatten for even baking.

4. Bake for 20 to 30 minutes, using a large spatula (to avoid breaking the chunks) to flip the granola every 10 minutes until the granola looks dry. Let cool on the baking sheets. The granola will crisp as it cools. If it isn't crisp to your liking once cool, bake again.

5. Let cool completely before storing in an airtight container at room temperature, or in the refrigerator, for up to 2 weeks.

Yield: 6½ cups (about 28 ounces, or 800 g)

PLANET SAVER TIP 4

Make your own nut milk to control what goes in it! The nut pulp left over from straining the milk can be used in oatmeal, tofu or chickpea scrambles, soups, or smoothies.

Combine 2 cups (280 g) raw cashews or almonds with enough filtered water to cover. Cover the container and soak overnight at room temperature or in the refrigerator. Drain the nuts (reserve the soaking water for your outdoors plants), give them a quick rinse, and combine with 3 cups (720 ml) filtered water and a pinch of kosher salt in a blender. Blend on high speed until perfectly smooth. You can add a pitted date for sweetness or more water for a thinner milk. Use a nut milk bag to strain the milk thoroughly. If using a high-speed blender, there might be no pulp left at all. Refrigerate in a glass bottle with an airtight lid for up to 3 days. Shake the bottle before each use. Yield: 3 to 4 cups (720 to 960 ml)

BREAKFAST RICE PUDDING

 GF **SF** Finding yourself with a huge amount of plain cooked rice but you'd rather not go for fried rice again? If you like your breakfast to be filling and healthy, this is a good option that's also fairly fast to prepare.

1½ cups (300 g) cooked jasmine rice

1 can (13.5-ounce, or 400 ml) full-fat coconut milk, or half coconut milk and half plant-based milk of choice

1 to 2 tablespoons (12 to 24 g) sweetener of choice, or to taste (optional)

Pinch Diamond kosher salt

2 cups (390 g) chopped hulled strawberries

⅓ cup (60 g) pomegranate seeds

2 tablespoons (40 g) pomegranate molasses

2 cups (420 g) chopped fresh pineapple

1 tablespoon (15 ml) fresh lemon juice

1 tablespoon (20 g) agave nectar

1 teaspoon golden milk powder, or ¼ teaspoon ground turmeric and ½ teaspoon ground ginger

Diced crystallized ginger, chopped vegan halva, toasted coconut flakes, toasted cashew nuts, fresh mint leaves, for garnish

1. In a saucepan over medium-high heat, combine the cooked rice, coconut milk, sweetener (if using), and salt. Cover the pan and bring to a boil. Lower the heat slightly and simmer until creamy and thickened, about 10 minutes, stirring occasionally.

2. In the meantime, and about 30 minutes before eating the pudding, have two medium-size bowls handy. Place the strawberries and pomegranate seeds in one. Pour the molasses on top and gently fold to combine. Set aside.

3. In the other bowl, combine the pineapple, lemon juice, agave, and milk powder. Gently fold to combine. Set aside.

4. The rice pudding can be eaten warm, at room temperature, or cold. Once ready to eat, serve the pudding in bowls. Generously top with the fruit mixture of choice and garnishes of choice.

Yield: 3 servings

PLANET SAVER TIP 5

No one wants to throw away food they've spent time and energy preparing. And no one wants to get sick because of their food, either! Here's a fact about rice I never knew until I was well into my thirties. It's important to refrigerate rice within 1 hour of being cooked because of a bacterium called Bacillus cereus. The heat-resistant spores of this bacteria can sometimes be found in dry foods that grow close to or in the ground and will germinate once the dry food is combined with moisture. Note that the refrigeration process doesn't kill the bacteria (my goodness, this thing just won't die!) but does slow its growth, which is why the lifespan of refrigerated cooked rice should be no longer than 3 days for safest eating. Of course, it is best to store only cooled foods in the refrigerator. I usually spread cooked rice on a large plate so it cools faster.

SOURED-OAT HAND WAFFLES

What do I mean by "hand waffle?" It's the kind of waffle that doesn't need syrup or nut butter or anything added to it to shine. You can just toast it and enjoy it on the go, on your way to wherever, without getting messy.

1 tablespoon (10.5 g) whole flaxseed, ground

3 tablespoons (45 ml) water

1 cup (240 ml) kombucha or plant-based milk of choice

⅓ cup (80 ml) roasted peanut, walnut, or hazelnut oil or oil of choice

½ cup (72 g) coconut sugar, (96 g) Sucanat, or (75 g) light brown sugar

4 ounces (115 g) sourdough discard from the fridge (see Planet Saver Tip 11, page 40)

1 teaspoon golden milk powder, or ¼ teaspoon ground turmeric and ½ teaspoon ground ginger

1 teaspoon ground cinnamon

½ teaspoon Diamond kosher salt

1½ cups (180 g) all-purpose flour or whole-wheat pastry flour

1 cup (80 g) old-fashioned rolled oats

2 teaspoons baking powder

½ cup (75 g) raisins (optional)

½ cup (60 g) dry-roasted walnut halves, coarsely chopped (optional)

Oil spray

1. In a large bowl, whisk to combine the flaxseed and water. Let stand for 5 minutes to thicken.

2. Add the kombucha, oil, coconut sugar, sourdough discard, milk powder, cinnamon, and salt. Whisk to combine.

3. In a medium-size bowl, whisk to combine the flour, oats, and baking powder. Stir the dry ingredients into the wet ingredients just until combined. Fold in the raisins (if using) and walnuts just to combine. Let stand for 15 minutes while preheating the waffle iron.

4. Preheat the waffle iron according to the manufacturer's instructions. Once heated, lightly coat it with oil spray and add the quantity of batter recommended by the manufacturer (usually ¼ to ½ cup, or 60 to 120 g, depending on the size of your iron). Cook until golden brown and crisp, about 6 minutes. Cook time will also vary by machine. Repeat with the remaining batter.

5. Refrigerate leftovers in an airtight container for up to 4 days, or freeze for up to 1 month. To reheat, toast in a 325°F (170°C, or gas mark 3) oven or toaster oven until crisp again, about 10 minutes.

Yield: about 12 waffles

PLANET SAVER TIP 6

Want to replace actual eggs with flax eggs? They're my favorite way to veganize egg-loaded recipes. I purchase golden flaxseed as they are a little less noticeable in lighter-colored baked goods. Look for whole seeds versus pre-milled ones and keep them in the freezer or refrigerator: flaxseed is rich in natural oils, which are known to have a blast going rancid very quickly. Grinding them as needed and storing them somewhere cool ensures you won't end up throwing your money in the trash.

BREAKFAST GREEÑA COLADA

   Relax: there's no booze in the breakfast version of the popular exotic cocktail! Simply lots of fruit and enough nutrition to make it part of a morning meal to get you on your way.

1 cup (210 g) chopped frozen pineapple

1 frozen banana, chopped (no peel)

1 cup (60 g) packed fresh baby spinach or (67 g) kale leaves

1 cup (240 ml) fresh orange juice

1 cup (240 ml) plain or vanilla plant-based milk of choice

2 tablespoons (28 g) coconut manna, or ¼ cup (60 g) plain coconut yogurt

1 tablespoon (15 ml) fresh lime juice

In a blender, combine all the ingredients. Blend on high speed until perfectly smooth. Serve immediately.

Yield: 2 servings

PLANET SAVER TIP 7

If using kale for this recipe, remove the leaves from the stem but, for the love of all that is green, do not discard the stems! Wash them separately, spin them dry, and use them in salads or sauté with other vegetables. I love to chop them just a bit and throw them in the food processor to pulse into a riced/confetti state like one would do with cauliflower. It's a great raw addition to big bowls of mixed vegetable salads. The same can be done with broccoli stems (use a vegetable peeler to remove and compost any part that is way too hard for consumption) and carrots.

PINK LATTE

FF **GF** **SF** This pink-hued beverage is the perfect pick-me-up for the traditional mid-morning or post-lunch energy drop you might experience in these crazy times. I usually reserve strawberries that are a little less than, how to put it, spotless for such applications. You know the ones: a little squishy but perfectly tasty. If you don't have coconut manna, you can replace ⅓ cup (80 ml) of hot water with canned coconut milk for added creaminess and flavor.

¼ cup (42.5 g) chopped
fresh strawberries

1½ teaspoons ground dried
hibiscus flower, or to taste

2 to 4 organic culinary-grade
rose buds

3 tablespoons (42 g)
coconut manna

1 to 2 pitted dates, or to taste

1 cup (240 ml) hot water

In a blender, combine all the ingredients. Blend on high speed until perfectly smooth. Serve immediately.

Yield: 1 serving

**PLANET
SAVER TIP
8**

I use coconut manna quite often, but you might wonder what it is, if you're not familiar with it. It's simply coconut flesh blended into a buttery, creamy paste that can be used as a spread, added to smoothies or soups, and much more for added flavor and nutrition. You can make your own by processing a bag of unsweetened coconut flakes or shredded coconut, allowing the food processor to work on releasing the oils from the coconut flesh just like making nut butter. The resulting paste can be stored in a sealed jar at room temperature for up to 1 month.

PINEAPPLE BERRY SWIRL SMOOTHIE

FF While smoothies are a good alternative to more substantial breakfast meals for those of us who don't have much of an appetite early in the day, they also make a great snack or cocktail for anyone who wants to celebrate in an alcohol-free way. The quick jam for this smoothie also makes a glorious fiber-rich topping for Plain Jane Sourdough Waffles (page 40) or Breakfast Rice Pudding (page 32).

**FOR OVERNIGHT
STRAWBERRY CHIA JAM**

2 cups (390 g) chopped
hulled strawberries

⅓ cup (60 g) pomegranate seeds

2 tablespoons (40 g)
pomegranate molasses

2 tablespoons (20 g) chia seeds

FOR SMOOTHIE

1 cup (210 g) chopped
frozen pineapple

1 cup (240 g) overnight
strawberry chia jam (recipe
above), blended smooth

1 cup (240 ml) plain or vanilla
plant-based milk of choice

1 tablespoon (16 g) cashew butter
or (14 g) coconut manna

1 tablespoon (5 g) old-fashioned
rolled oats

1. To make the overnight strawberry chia jam: In a medium-size bowl, combine the strawberries and pomegranate seeds. Pour the molasses on top and gently fold to combine. Add the chia seeds, stir well, and refrigerate overnight to thicken.

2. To make the smoothie: In the blender, combine all the ingredients. Blend on high speed until perfectly smooth. Serve immediately.

Yield: 2 servings plus about 2 cups (480 g) jam

PLANET
SAVER TIP
9

Got leftover porridge you just can't finish? Or maybe some nut pulp leftover from making your own milk? Use either (or both) here instead of the rolled oats to bring bulk and nutrition to your smoothie. I also love to use leftover nut pulp in tofu or chickpea breakfast scrambles. Just remove unwanted moisture by patting it dry with a clean reusable towel, then sauté in oil with the tofu or chickpeas. The pulp adds bulk and nutrition and a little bit more of that scrambled-egg look and texture.

BAKED SWEET POTATO BREAD

 Not only do you get to use up leftover baked potatoes and stale beer with this recipe, but, dang, if it isn't some of the loveliest bread, too!

1 medium-size (7 ounces, or 200 g) baked sweet potato with skin on, lukewarm or at room temperature

2½ cups (300 g) all-purpose or bread flour, plus more as needed

1 teaspoon fast-acting yeast

¾ cup (180 ml) stale vegan beer, lukewarm or at room temperature

2 tablespoons (30 ml) roasted walnut oil or extra-virgin olive oil

1 tablespoon (20 g) blackstrap molasses

2 teaspoons Diamond kosher salt

⅓ cup (49 g) roasted and salted sunflower seeds or other seeds or nuts of choice

1. In a large bowl, combine all the ingredients except the sunflower seeds, making sure the yeast and salt don't touch. Stir with a silicone spatula or wooden spoon (if hand-kneading), or use a stand mixer fitted with the dough hook, until well-combined. Transfer to a well-floured work surface if hand-kneading. Add more flour, as needed, so the dough is not too sticky. Note that if using a stand mixer, you won't need to add quite as much flour as if hand-kneading.

2. Knead the dough for about 5 minutes by hand, or 4 minutes in the mixer. Add the sunflower seeds and knead for about 5 minutes more by hand, or 4 minutes more by mixer to incorporate. The dough should be smooth and not too sticky. Place or leave in a large bowl, loosely cover with a clean towel, and let rise until doubled in size, about 2 hours, depending on the room temperature.

3. Uncover, and gently punch down the dough. Shape the dough into 1 or 2 round loaves and place them into floured bannetons (bread-shaping baskets), if using. Otherwise place the shaped dough on a piece of parchment paper. Loosely cover with a clean towel and let rise until doubled in size, about 1 hour.

4. Preheat the oven to 450°F (232°C, or gas mark 8).

5. Place a large Dutch oven (or two smaller ones, if available, as long as the bread or breads fit in what you have without touching) in the oven while it preheats.

6. Gently transfer the dough from the bannetons onto a piece of parchment paper. Use a lame or a sharp knife to make shallow cuts on top of the bread to allow for expansion.

7. Carefully transfer the loaves into the heated Dutch oven(s), cover, and bake for 30 minutes.

8. Remove the lid(s) and bake for another 15 minutes, or until dark golden brown and the bottoms sound hollow when tapped. Let cool completely before slicing.

Yield: 1 big loaf or 2 smaller ones

PLANET SAVER TIP 10

Making extra baked sweet potatoes is always a good idea. You get to bulk up future meals or make bread, like this one, and as an added bonus, your huge oven doesn't waste its energy baking just a couple of lonely potatoes.

PLAIN JANE SOURDOUGH WAFFLES

SF If you're amongst the folks who really (really) got into baking sourdough bread during the recent pandemic, you are aware of the starter discard involved with every feeding. And you, too, probably cannot bear the thought of tossing perfectly good ingredients in the trash. So, instead of fretting, make sourdough waffles.

1 cup (120 g) all-purpose or whole-wheat pastry flour

2 teaspoons baking powder

¾ cup (180 ml) stale vegan beer, kombucha, or water

4 ounces (115 g) sourdough starter discard from the fridge

¼ cup (60 ml) olive oil or other neutral-flavored oil

2 tablespoons (21 g) whole flaxseed, ground

2 tablespoons (24 g) sweetener of choice

¾ teaspoon Diamond kosher salt

1 tablespoon (15 ml) apple cider vinegar

Oil spray

1. In a medium-size bowl, sift together the flour and baking powder. Set aside.

2. In a large bowl, whisk to combine the remaining ingredients, except the oil spray. Add the flour mixture to the wet ingredients and stir until just combined. Let stand for 15 minutes while preheating the waffle iron.

3. Preheat the waffle iron according to the manufacturer's instructions. Once heated, lightly coat with oil spray and add the quantity of batter recommended by the manufacturer (usually ¼ to ½ cup, or 60 to 120 g, depending on size of your iron). Cook until golden brown and crisp, about 6 minutes. Cook time will also vary by machine. Repeat with the remaining batter.

4. Refrigerate leftovers in an airtight container for up to 4 days, or freeze for up to 1 month. To reheat, toast in a 325°F (170°C, or gas mark 3) oven or toaster oven until crisp again, about 10 minutes.

Yield: about 10 waffles

PLANET SAVER TIP 11

Sourdough discard is basically an even combination of flour and water. Therefore, it's fairly easy to replace some of the flour and water from a baked goods recipe, such as crackers or even cake, with it. It's best not to replace an ingredient that has a specific purpose in a recipe (for example, plant-based milk to bring softness and a little fat), so stick to using the discard in recipes that include flour and water. For example, say you have 6 ounces (170 g) of sourdough discard. You will need to replace 3 ounces (85 g) of flour and 3 ounces (90 ml) of water in the recipe with the discard. It gets a little trickier with odd amounts, but that's probably why they made us study mathematics when we were wee.

THE WHOLE LEMON CURD

GF **SF** Do you like things to be a touch tart in the morning? I have just what you need. Ideal for spreading on toast, pancakes, and waffles—even muffins. This curd makes good use of your organic lemons—not using just the zest and juice, but the whole dang thing instead. Adjust the amount of tartness by adding more (or less) sweetener. It won't change the texture one bit.

1 large organic lemon, scrubbed clean

½ cup (112 g) coconut manna

½ cup (120 ml) water

½ to ¾ cup (160 to 240 g) agave nectar

1 tablespoon (8 g) organic cornstarch

1. In a blender, combine all the ingredients and process on high speed until smooth. Transfer to a medium-size saucepan over medium-high heat and bring to a low boil. Lower the heat and simmer until thickened like a yogurt, about 10 minutes, whisking frequently and adjusting the heat as needed. Let cool in the saucepan for a few minutes, whisking occasionally to prevent a "skin" from forming. Transfer to a heat-safe jar.

2. Refrigerate, covered, for up to 3 weeks. Note that the curd will thicken further once cooled.

Yield: 1 pint (480 ml)

PLANET SAVER TIP 12

If you have trees in your yard that yield fruit, you are lucky! We see so many people in town with trees loaded with oranges, lemons, apricots, avocados . . . you name it, it is there. Yet they fail to do the picking part and the produce ends up rotting away at the foot of the tree. Here's an idea: You don't want it, it's your right! But how about offering the goods to anyone interested? Either sell it for a small fee if you don't want to give it away (I'm not judging), or have those who want it pick it themselves. Another option is to pick it and place bags full in the front yard with a For Free sign. Your yard won't smell like rotten fruit and attract swarms of wasps and you'll have earned a massive amount of karma points with that small action.

LEMON CURD MUFFINS

A not-so-distant relative of pound cake, these treats showcase a proud bakery-style muffin top like any self-respecting muffin should. They make good use of The Whole Lemon Curd (page 41). Add extra curd upon serving if you want to pucker up. The tartness of raspberry jam would also make a delightful addition here. If you want smaller muffins without a big top, make seven or eight, instead of six. Keep an eye for doneness, though, as smaller muffins will need less time in the oven: check after 18 to 20 minutes.

Oil spray, optional

1 cup (120 g) organic powdered sugar

4 candied dried lemon slices, chopped

¼ cup (60 ml) extra-virgin olive oil

¼ cup (60 ml) roasted walnut oil or more extra-virgin olive oil

1 tablespoon (12 g) white chia seeds

½ cup (120 g) The Whole Lemon Curd (page 41)

½ cup (120 g) plain, vanilla, or lemon plant-based yogurt

½ teaspoon Diamond kosher salt

1½ cups (180 g) all-purpose flour

2 teaspoons baking powder

1. Peheat the oven to 350°F (180°C, or gas mark 4). Line 6 wells of a standard muffin tin with (recycled, preferably) paper liners, or lightly coat the pan with oil instead.

2. In a small food processor or blender, combine the sugar, chopped dried lemon, oils, chia seeds, lemon curd, yogurt, and salt. Process until mostly smooth.

3. Sift the flour and baking powder into a medium-size bowl. Add the liquid ingredients to the dry ingredients and stir until just combined. Divide the batter among the prepared tin wells.

4. Bake until golden brown on top, about 26 minutes. Place the tin on a cooling rack for a few minutes before removing the muffins from the tin. Serve with jam of choice or extra curd, as desired.

5. Refrigerate leftovers in an airtight container for up to 3 days. These muffins taste great warm, at room temperature, or chilled.

Yield: 6 muffins

PLANET SAVER TIP 13

Although it is necessary to preheat your oven for anything baking related, it's actually not mandatory for roasting vegetables or baking potatoes. Save a couple of cents on your electricity bill by popping them into the cold oven while it preheats—but do keep an eye open for readiness cues a few minutes early, as all recipes assume you will use a preheated oven, for convention's sake.

AB & FERMENTED J POTS DE CRÈME

GF Maybe you want to treat yourself to something healthy but a little fancier for breakfast today. You deserve it after the turmoil the world has seen recently. Make this recipe a couple of days before serving to allow the berries to ferment and the crème to thicken.

FOR BERRIES

8 ounces (225 g) fresh blueberries, rinsed and patted dry

1 tablespoon (15 ml) fresh lime or lemon juice

¾ teaspoon Diamond kosher salt

FOR POTS DE CRÈME

¾ cup (180 ml) coconut milk

½ cup (120 g) Labneh (page 127)

¼ cup (65 g) natural almond butter

¼ cup (48 g) Sucanat

Pinch Diamond kosher salt

1 teaspoon agar powder

1. To make the berries: In a medium-size bowl, combine the blueberries, lime juice, and salt. Transfer to a small sterilized glass jar fitted with an airtight lid, pressing down gently on the berries. Add a small weight on top (a piece of cheesecloth with a few pie weights in it, for example). Place a piece of cheesecloth on the opening, and loosely close the lid. Allow the berries to ferment at room temperature for 1 to 2 days until they puff up a little and smell pleasantly sour. The time it will take will depend on the temperature. Refrigerate until ready to use, for up to 1 week.

2. To make the pots de crème: In a medium-size bowl, whisk to blend the coconut milk, labneh, almond butter, Sucanat, and salt until smooth. Transfer to a medium-size saucepan over medium-high heat. Whisk the agar into the mixture. Bring to a low boil, lower the heat to medium, and cook for 5 minutes to activate and dissolve the agar. Whisk frequently and cook for 2 minutes more. Pour the crème into 2 heat-safe half-pint jars and let cool. Refrigerate for at least 4 hours, or ideally overnight.

3. Serve with the berries and whipped coconut cream, if desired.

Yield: 2 servings

PLANET SAVER TIP 14

If you ever come across nuts in bulk with a winning price, bag yourself a bunch and make your own nut butter. I've made batches in a not-so-stellar food processor in the past, it just takes a while and needs frequent breaks to let the motor catch its breath. If you have one of those fancy high-speed blenders, needless to say, this will go a little faster. You can add salt to taste, a touch of matching oil, if needed, to move things along: roasted walnut oil for walnut butter, roasted peanut oil for peanut butter, etc. Regular oils, like canola, olive, or grapeseed, are fine, too. And, of course, use raw or roasted nuts according to your preference. Refrigerate the resulting nut butter in glass jars for up to 1 month.

OVERNIGHT GRANOLA BOWL

So easy to make, this recipe's a favorite of mine for a satisfying first meal of the day, or when a snack is a must. Think of overnight oats, but already packing in all the flavor for you. You can keep it healthy by picking unsweetened yogurt and milk and using a jam or compote with very little or even no sugar.

½ cup (120 g) unsweetened plain plant-based yogurt of choice

¼ cup (60 ml) unsweetened plain plant-based milk of choice

Heaping ½ cup (135 g) Chunky Nut Granola (page 31), Beer Nut Granola (48) or granola of choice

Jam, compote, or fruit of choice, for serving

1. In a small bowl, fold together the yogurt, milk, and granola. Cover and refrigerate overnight.

2. Top with jam when ready to serve.

Yield: 1 serving

PLANET SAVER TIP 15

Do you remember that liquid you set aside when making Labneh (page 127)? The equivalent of dairy whey, sans dairy? Right. Use it here instead of some or all of the milk! You can also use the pulp left over from making milk (see Planet Saver Tip 4, page 31) if you'd like, to further bulk up this breakfast bowl. If you want to make an Instagram-worthy looker of a bowl, use a little star-shaped cookie cutter to cut banana slices into stars and garnish the bowl. A mixture of toasted seeds (chia, flax, poppy, etc.) also makes a pretty picture when scattered across the bowl.

BANANA BERRY SMOOTHIE BOWL

FF **GF** A healthy frozen treat, designed for breakfast-y goodness! If you have other berries that found their way into the freezer, use them instead of blueberries. Anything goes here. You can also add a small handful of fresh baby spinach leaves—if you fancy. This will alter the resulting color somewhat, but it will also add nutritional value. If using milk that is certified soy-free, the SF recipe label applies here.

1 frozen banana, chopped

6 ounces (170 g) frozen blueberries

1 to 2 tablespoons (16 to 32 g) natural almond butter, or to taste, plus more for topping

Plant-based milk of choice or flavored or plain sparkling water (coconut works well), as needed

Fresh berries, banana stars, granola, seeds, toasted nuts, for topping

1. Place a bowl in the freezer while preparing the recipe.

2. In a high-speed blender or food processor, combine the banana, blueberries, and almond butter. Process on high speed until smooth, using a tamper to push down on the ingredients if using a blender, and if available. Add a splash of milk or sparkling water as needed if the machine struggles to process the ingredients. Transfer to the chilled bowl, add toppings of choice, and serve immediately.

Yield: 1 serving

PLANET SAVER TIP 16

This is another recipe where the Labneh (page 127) whey can be used instead of milk, and the milk-making pulp (see Planet Saver Tip 4, page 31) can be added to bulk up nutritional value. Remember to use reusable silicone bags to freeze your bananas! Silicone bags can be washed in the dishwasher and towel-dried to avoid water spots. It's great to use a bottlebrush, if washing by hand, with gentle dish liquid to make sure every corner is spotless. And if smells are troublesome, soak in a 50/50 mixture of warm water and vinegar before washing with detergent and the aforementioned bottlebrush. Note that most brands of silicone bags should not be turned inside out when cleaning or drying because this could damage them.

TRAIL MIX COOKIES

I love to eat energy bars for my first meal, before going for a long, fast walk. It gives me lots of pep without weighing me down. But I also love to know what goes into what I eat, so baking healthier cookies is the way to go when time permits. These cookies are perfect with their various textures and amazing flavor. It's definitely a recipe that begs for improvisation according to what you have and want. So, play around with it, by all means.

¼ cup (42 g) golden whole flaxseed, ground

½ cup (75 g) raisins

½ cup (72 g) roasted salted sunflower seeds

½ cup (60 g) vegan granola of choice

½ cup (60 g) whole-wheat flour

½ cup (96 g) Sucanat, (72 g) coconut sugar, or (75 g) light brown sugar (not packed)

½ cup (60 g) almond meal

½ teaspoon baking powder

½ teaspoon ground cinnamon

¼ cup (60 ml) roasted walnut oil or other oil

¼ cup (60 ml) coconut, or other flavor, sparkling water or plant-based milk of choice, plus more as needed

1. Preheat the oven to 350°F (180°C, or gas mark 4). Line a baking sheet with a silicone baking mat.

2. In a large bowl, stir to combine the flaxseed, raisins, sunflower seeds, granola, flour, Sucanat, almond meal, baking powder, and cinnamon. Pour in the walnut oil and stir a couple of times to partially incorporate. Add 2 tablespoons (30 ml) of coconut water, stir well, and add the remaining 2 tablespoons (30 ml) of water, if needed, and more as needed to make a dough that is neither too dry nor too wet. Pack a large cookie scoop with dough (¼ cup, or 80 g per cookie), and place on the prepared baking sheet. Flatten a little and neaten up the rounded shape of the cookie. They will puff a little and spread just slightly while baking. Repeat with the remaining dough.

3. Bake until light golden brown, about 16 minutes. Transfer to a cooling rack and enjoy, preferably, the day of baking. If you don't want to bake the whole batch in one shot, refrigerate the dough in an airtight container for up to 3 days and bake as needed.

Yield: 8 large cookies

PLANET SAVER TIP 17

Summers are long over here in our part of California. We drink flavored sparkling water as if our lives depended on it. Which, I suppose, they kind of do. Anyway, we occasionally try new flavors that aren't always a win. Such as the coconut flavor used here. The point I'm trying to make is that if you purchase something you're not a fan of, don't be afraid to get creative and use it in recipes where the flavor will be less in the forefront, and therefore, less noticed but still useful and, you guessed it—not wasted.

HALVA SCONES

On a whim, I purchased way too many blocks of vegan halva in a recent online order. I mean, sometimes you have to reach a certain price to get free shipping and I'm nothing if not a tightwad! I've been trying to use it all up before it mummifies in my refrigerator. Can't go wrong by pairing it in breakfast pastries, with a bit of sourdough discard thrown in for tasty good measure. If halva isn't available, use another favorite sweet of yours. Marzipan would be nice.

1 cup (120 g) all-purpose or whole-wheat pastry flour

3 tablespoons (24 g) roasted white sesame seeds or chopped roasted pistachios

⅓ cup (67 g) granulated pure cane sugar

2 teaspoons baking powder

½ teaspoon Diamond kosher salt

¼ cup (56 g) coconut oil or vegan butter

About ½ cup plus 2 tablespoons (170 g) sourdough discard from the fridge

3 ounces (85 g) chopped vegan halva

Plant-based milk, as needed, for mixing

1. Preheat the oven to 375°F (190°C, or gas mark 5). Line a baking sheet with a silicone baking mat.

2. In a food processor, combine the flour, sesame seeds, sugar, baking powder, and salt. Pulse a few times to combine. Add the oil, sourdough discard, and halva. Pulse a few times to distribute evenly. The dough should just hold together when pinched. If it is too dry, add a few drops of plant-based milk, as needed, very little at a time. If it is too wet, the scones will spread out quite a lot while baking and look more cookie-like than scone-ish, so don't be too generous!

3. Transfer the dough to the prepared baking sheet and shape it into a 6-inch (15 cm) disk. Pat it down slightly and cut the disk into 6 equal triangles. Pat down each scone slightly, separating them from each other.

4. Bake until light golden brown, 14 to 16 minutes. Transfer to a cooling rack to cool before eating.

Yield: 6 scones

PLANET
SAVER TIP
18

The best way to store flour if you are a frequent baker is to place it in the largest Mason jars you can find, fitted with airtight lids. They are fairly affordable, reusable, and not an eyesore either. They should be placed in a dark cupboard, ideally, for longest storage. If you aren't a frequent baker though, I recommend popping what you don't use in the freezer or refrigerator and taking out what you need a few hours before use. Technically, newly purchased flour should be popped into the freezer or refrigerator no matter what to kill potential bugs that might have come with the purchase. Neat. It's a bit of a pain as it calls for short-term extra refrigerator room a lot of us don't seem to have. Regardless, I do this every single time and am happy to report I've been pantry bug-free since I started. I wish you the same luck.

BEER NUT GRANOLA

SF I gave you Salty Beer Caramel Sauce (page 50); now let's work on using it up. Not that you really need any other way than just pouring it on top of your waffles, pancakes, and ice cream. The boozy smell of the granola is intoxicating (not literally) while it bakes. Beer (flavor) for breakfast? Don't mind if we do.

1½ cups (weight varies) raw nuts of choice (cashews, peanuts, pecans, or walnuts)

1¼ cups (100 g) old-fashioned rolled oats

¼ cup (30 g) unsweetened coconut flakes

¼ cup (41 g) buckwheat groats

1 cup (240 ml) Salty Beer Caramel Sauce (page 50)

2 tablespoons (30 ml) roasted or regular peanut oil

1 teaspoon Diamond kosher salt

1. Preheat the oven to 275°F (140°C, or gas mark 1). Line a large rimmed sheet pan with a silicone baking mat or parchment paper.

2. In a large bowl, stir together all the ingredients and spread in an even layer on the prepared baking sheet.

3. Bake for 1 hour, or until golden brown and dry, flipping the granola every 10 minutes. Avoid stirring so that the clumps don't break apart too much. The granola will crisp as it cools, but if you find it's not crisp enough once cooled, pop it back in the oven for a little bit longer, 5 to 10 minutes. Let cool.

4. Store in an airtight container at room temperature, or the refrigerator, for up to 2 weeks.

Yield: 5 cups (about 21 ounces, or 600 g)

PLANET SAVER TIP 19

I love adding granola to quick breads, muffins, waffles, or pancakes. It adds bulk, flavor, and let's not forget, an extra layer of awesomeness to pretty much anything you want to throw it in. This granola can also be built according to what nuts, seeds, and oils you have at the bottom of your bags and bottles: mixing and matching is absolutely fine if it allows you to put all of these to rest and start anew. Just don't use small seeds, like sesame or poppy, which would more than likely burn in the oven. And for the oil, choose something toasted or not, but still neutral. Don't go with toasted sesame oil, for example. That would be a little too savory here.

SALTY BEER CARAMEL SAUCE

SF Celebration night was a hoot, but now you find yourself with a couple of opened beer bottles you just can't bring yourself to pour in the sink? Don't fret. Make caramel instead. (But, uhm . . . make sure you know who put their lips on the beer bottles and don't grab a complete stranger's just for the sake of making caramel. It's not worth it.) Note that you can use any type of vegan beer you prefer, but bear in mind that the stronger the beer, the stronger its taste will pop in the caramel. And if you have no stale beer leftovers? Crack open a new one. The bubbles aren't a problem at all. Hair of the dog, caramel-style. Apply liberally on Plain Jane Sourdough Waffles (page 40), or pancakes, or make Beer Nut Granola (page 48).

1½ cups plus 1 tablespoon (300 g) Sucanat or (234 g) dark brown sugar

1½ cups (360 ml) stale vegan lager beer

Scant 1 cup (235 ml) coconut cream (only the white part from a can of full-fat milk; reserve the remaining liquid)

1 teaspoon Diamond kosher salt

1. In a medium-size saucepan over medium-high heat, combine all the ingredients and bring to a boil, stirring to dissolve the sugar crystals, about 1 minute. Lower the heat to medium and continue to cook until the bubbling mixture reaches 230°F (110°C) on a candy thermometer, using a pastry brush to brush sugar crystals from the sides of the saucepan, as needed, and the sauce has reduced to half its original amount. It should be thickened and glossy. This will take about 1 hour.

2. Let cool completely, whisking occasionally. Refrigerate in an airtight container overnight before use; the caramel will thicken as it cools. Keep refrigerated for up to 3 weeks.

Yield: 1 pint (480 ml)

PLANET SAVER TIP 20

Halt. Do not throw away the watery part of the can of coconut milk. It can be used in so many ways: to cook rice and puddings, added to soups, hummus, smoothies, porridge . . . the list is pretty much endless. Pretty handy considering cans of coconut milk can be fairly costly depending on your brand of choice.

MISO CARAMEL SPREAD

FF I'm always looking for fun stuff to spread on my Soured-Oat Hand Waffles (page 34), The Whole Banana-nola Bread (page 52), and toast. When I found myself drowning under tests and more tests for the Salty Beer Caramel Sauce (page 50), I figured it was time to come up with creative ways to use it all up rather than just pouring it in my gullet. Behold, this thick, spreadable, salty-sweet spread. Insider tip: it's pretty good slathered on apple slices and bananas, too.

2 Medjool dates, pitted

1½ tablespoons (23 ml) hot water

6 tablespoons (90 ml) Salty Beer Caramel Sauce (page 50)

1 tablespoon (20 g) white miso

¼ cup (56 g) coconut manna

1 tablespoon (15 ml) roasted peanut oil or other nut oil, or (14 g) coconut oil

1. In a small bowl, combine the dates and hot water. Let soak for 5 minutes. Drain and transfer to a small food processor.

2. Add the remaining ingredients and process on high speed until smooth, stopping to scrape the sides once or twice, as needed.

3. Refrigerate, covered, for up to 2 weeks.

Yield: ¾ cup (260 g)

PLANET SAVER TIP 21

If you don't have reusable BPA-free storage bowls with lids to contain your leftovers, consider purchasing linen and/or cotton bowl covers, airtight silicone lids (such as Five Two from Food52), or even vegan wax food wraps (such as Khala Cloths) that can be molded on top of regular bowls with the heat of one's hands and reused repeatedly provided they are cared for properly. That way you avoid using cling paper and aluminum foil, or making do with a non-airtight plate on top of a bowl for (precarious) protection.

THE WHOLE BANANA—NOLA BREAD

You, too, will now see the "a-peel" of using the whole banana in your bread rather than just the flesh. Just make sure you use a super-duper ripe banana so the flavor pops.

Oil spray (optional)

1 large (about 10 ounces, or 300 g) ripe organic banana, with skin, scrubbed clean, patted dry

½ cup (120 ml) plant-based milk of choice

⅓ cup (80 ml) olive oil or other neutral-flavored oil

1½ cups plus 1 tablespoon (188 g) all-purpose flour

¾ cup (150 g) granulated pure cane sugar

1 tablespoon (8 g) organic cornstarch

2 teaspoons baking powder

½ teaspoon Diamond kosher salt

1 cup (120 g) vegan granola of choice, large chunks broken down a bit

1. Preheat the oven to 350°F (180°C, or gas mark 4). Lightly coat an 8 × 4-inch (20 × 10 cm) loaf pan with oil spray, or line it with parchment paper. Alternatively, bake the bread in an 8-inch (20 cm) round pan with a quicker baking time for an energy-saving move.

2. In a blender, combine the banana, milk, and oil. Process until smooth.

3. In a large bowl, whisk to combine the flour, sugar, and cornstarch. Pour the banana mixture in the dry ingredients and stir a few times just to combine. Fold in the granola. Pour the batter into the prepared loaf pan.

4. Bake for 50 to 60 minutes until a toothpick inserted into the center comes out clean. If you baked the bread in a round pan, check for doneness after 35 minutes. Place the pan on a cooling rack. Let cool in the pan for 10 minutes before removing the bread. Let cool completely before slicing. Store leftovers in an airtight tin at room temperature, or in the refrigerator, for up to 2 days. Enjoy toasted or as is, with a smear of nut butter, vegan butter, or Miso Caramel Spread (page 51).

Yield: 8 servings

PLANET SAVER TIP 22

Does the idea of using the banana peel freak you out a bit? It's been done in various parts of the world for the longest time, so why not try it? Unless you are a compost aficionado, throwing away the peel feels like such a waste! It's loaded with banana flavor and absolutely fine to use in baked goods, provided you give it a good scrub to clean it, trim the tougher stem and bottom part, and, of course, go for organic.

BAKED BANANA NUT OATMEAL

GF Now that you realize using banana peels is not only perfectly okay, but actually quite tasty (see The Whole Banana-nola Bread, page 52), here's another recipe using them. I've always loved baked oatmeal more than the stove-top version, probably because of the caramelization and overall more-appealing texture. This version pairs bananas with nut butter and there's never anything wrong with that combination.

Oil spray

3 small ripe organic bananas with skin, scrubbed clean, patted dry

1 cup (240 ml) plant-based milk of choice

⅓ cup (86 g) natural peanut butter or other nut butter

1 tablespoon (15 ml) toasted peanut oil or other oil

1½ cups (120 g) old-fashioned rolled oats

¾ cup (90 g) almond meal

⅓ cup (weight varies) vegan semisweet chocolate chips, raisins, or chopped pitted dates

¼ cup (48 g) Sucanat, (36 g) coconut sugar, or (37.5 g) light brown sugar (not packed)

½ teaspoon Diamond kosher salt

1. Preheat the oven to 350°F (180°C, or gas mark 4). Lightly coat a 9-inch (23 cm) baking dish with oil spray.

2. In a blender, combine the bananas, milk, nut butter, and oil. Blend until smooth.

3. In a large bowl, combine the remaining ingredients. Pour the banana mixture on top and stir to combine. Let stand for 5 minutes before transferring the oatmeal to the prepared baking dish.

4. Bake until set and golden brown on top, about 25 minutes.

Yield: 4 servings

PLANET SAVER TIP 23

If you make your own plant-based milk but don't have a high-speed blender that will blend the nuts into oblivion, and, therefore, happen to have some soaked nut pulp leftover after straining the milk, incorporate it here! Nix ¼ cup (60 ml) milk and ¼ cup (30 g) almond meal from this recipe, replacing with ½ cup (weight varies, but about 120 g) of pulp.

CONGEE BOWL

Savory comfort food, in a bowl! While this rice porridge can be served for lunch or dinner, too, I wanted to offer it as a savory option for the first meal of the day. Some of us who have demanding jobs or workout regimens need a breakfast with a bit more bulk and calories than a muffin provides, and this should do the trick. Most of the dish can be prepared ahead and it can be adorned according to your preferences and needs. I like it with caramelized kimchi and pulled jackfruit on top. I broil them together, drizzled with just a hint of toasted sesame oil, and it takes just a few minutes to be ready, too.

1 cup (200 g) raw white jasmine rice

1 sheet dried kombu

7 cups (1.7 L) water, plus more as needed

1 tablespoon (15 ml) toasted sesame oil or peanut oil

1 head fermented black garlic (optional)

¾ cup (14 5) dried shiitake mushrooms

1½ cups (300 g) Fennel Kimchi (page 117) drained (brine reserved for another recipe) or store-bought vegan kimchi, gently squeezed dry

½ recipe pulled jackfruit (see Pulled Jackfruit Sandwiches, page 71)

Chopped scallion, white and green parts, for garnish

Soy sauce, for garnish

Roasted sesame seeds, for garnish

1. The night before cooking the congee, wash the rice in several rinses of water until the water is clear. Drain and transfer to a reusable storage bag or box. Freeze overnight, or up to several nights ahead.

2. When ready to prepare the congee, place the kombu sheet in a large pot and add the water. Let soak for 20 minutes. Place the pot over high heat and as soon as the water simmers, remove the kombu and set aside for other uses, or to freeze.

3. Add the oil, garlic, and rice to the water. Place the mushrooms on top and let soak for 5 to 10 minutes (depending on whether they are sliced or whole) to rehydrate. Remove and set aside to drain. (You can place the sieve on top of a bowl to keep the draining liquid, if desired.)

Recipe Continues

4. Cook the rice until thickened and porridge-like, about 20 minutes. Add more water if you want your congee to be even softer.

5. Preheat the broiler.

6. In a small baking dish, combine the kimchi and jackfruit. Broil for about 8 minutes until slightly caramelized at the edges.

7. Serve the congee in a bowl topped with the kimchi and jackfruit and any other garnishes, as desired.

8. Refrigerate cooled leftovers in an airtight container, and gently reheat during the rest of the week.

Yield: 6 servings

PLANET SAVER TIP 24

Kombu, the dark green seaweed filled with umami, minerals, and nutrients, is mainly used to make flavorful broth, also known as dashi. It shouldn't be washed or wiped before use and doesn't need to be discarded after making the dashi. If it is tender enough, I like to cut the sheet into very thin slices and add them to salads and soups. If it isn't tender enough, I usually reuse it to make another dashi until it is tender enough to be cut and enjoyed. Just be sure to store it in an airtight container and use it within 3 days if refrigerated, and 1 month if frozen.

FLAX CRACKERS

SF I'm a big fan of eating crisp bread-type crackers for breakfast, served with a generous layer of strawberry, raspberry, or other favorite jam for that sweet and salty lovin' feeling. Make sure the beer used is gluten-free and the GF icon will apply. Otherwise, sparkling water is a good replacement.

¾ cup (126 g) golden whole flaxseed, finely ground

¼ cup (30 g) almond meal

2 tablespoons (24 g) white whole chia seeds

1 tablespoon (8 g) toasted sesame seeds

1 tablespoon (15 g) maca powder

1½ teaspoons Diamond kosher salt

1 tablespoon (15 ml) roasted walnut oil or other oil

½ cup (120 ml) flat vegan lager beer or sparkling water

1. Preheat the oven to 300°F (150°C, or gas mark 2). Line a 9-inch (23 cm) square pan with parchment paper.

2. In a medium-size bowl, stir to combine the flaxseed, almond meal, chia seeds, sesame seeds, maca powder, and salt.

3. Add the oil and stir to combine.

4. Add the beer and stir again to combine. The mixture should be neither too wet, nor too dry. Transfer to the prepared pan. Use an angled spatula to spread the batter to the edges of the pan, making sure it is evenly flattened. You can score the cracker now for easier breaking once cooled, or leave as is for wilder-shaped shards.

5. Bake for 90 minutes, or until golden brown. Lower the heat to 250°F (130°C, or gas mark 1/2). Remove the sheet from the pan and flip the cracker upside-down. Bake for another 15 minutes. Let cool completely before breaking the cracker into shards to enjoy. Store in an airtight container at room temperature for up to 1 week.

Yield: 6 servings

PLANET SAVER TIP 25

Once you're done reading your morning newspaper while enjoying breakfast, if you haven't switched to reading your news online yet, set it aside and make sure to regularly add a shredded fistful to your compost bin—black-and-white pages only; it's generally advised not to recycle brightly colored paper. It will help absorb any excessive sogginess and keep things moving by adding carbon into the mix.

BARBECUE CHICKPEA SCRAMBLE

My go-to smoky scramble! I like it for the occasional breakfast if I'm in a savory mood, but it's just as great for quick evening meals and added to roasted vegetables and crudités bowls. If you don't have kale, use any greens that need to be urgently put to rest. Think beet greens, Swiss chard, even bok choy. As always, adjust cooking times according to the greens you have: you want them wilted, not cooked beyond redemption.

1 tablespoon (15 ml) toasted sesame oil

2¼ cups (371 g) cooked chickpeas

½ cup (65 g) minced rehydrated dried shiitake mushrooms (soaking liquid reserved)

1 large shallot, minced

½ teaspoon smoked sea salt, or to taste

½ cup (144 g) Sriracha Barbecue Sauce (page 65)

2 large garlic cloves, grated

3 cups (210 g) packed fresh kale leaves (stemmed, but stems reserved for another use)

1. In a large skillet over medium-high heat, combine the oil, chickpeas, mushrooms, shallot, and salt. Cook to brown slightly, about 2 minutes.

2. Stir in the barbecue sauce to combine. Cook until the sauce evaporates, about 6 minutes more, stirring occasionally.

3. Add the garlic and kale and cook just until wilted, about 4 minutes. Serve with toasted bread, on top of steamed rice, or as is, as desired.

Yield: 4 servings

PLANET SAVER TIP 26

Although dried mushrooms might appear a bit more costly than fresh, I find they are packed with even more umami goodness than their fresh counterpart. Their soaking liquid is also a treasure trove of flavor that can be used as a deglazing agent for other meals, or as part of the broth for your favorite bowl of soup. If you see a lot of sediment left after removing the mushrooms and giving them a gentle squeeze, filter the liquid in a sieve lined with cheesecloth. Refrigerate the resulting liquid in an airtight container for up to 3 days.

Savory Sweet
Cluck-Free Strips
Sandwiches
page 87

CHAPTER 3
MAIN COURSES

Putting the plant in plant-based like never before, this chapter is loaded with ideas to put this week's farmers' market loot to work. Most recipes can be altered to use whatever's in season and to suit your personal needs if you prefer x vegetable to the y used in such-and-such recipe. I readily admit it was a bit of a challenge to work without access to the local farmers' market due to the coronavirus pandemic and make do with the somewhat boring offerings from the supermarket instead. Most of us are more spoiled than we know (or care to admit) to usually get to cook with a far better produce selection. It's a good lesson in learning to appreciate the food on our plates now more than we used to, pre-Covid.

CHAAT MASALA PEAS AND QUINOA STEW

GF My cupboards are loaded with spice mixes facing a daily battle with dust bunnies. I really need to toss anything that's older than a year, but I'm loath to do it. That's why I like recipes that use a generous amount of said spice mixes so I never have to worry about throwing cash out the window. This one is comforting, while also being healthy and satisfying. I like to serve it with roasted vegetables, broccoli being my number one, followed by carrots. And cauliflower. Or kale chips. (Okay, so pretty much any roasted vegetable has my heart.)

2 tablespoons (30 ml) melted coconut oil

½ large yellow onion, chopped

2 tablespoons (40 g) red or white miso

2 garlic cloves, grated

2 tablespoons (10 g) nutritional yeast (powder)

1 tablespoon (6 g) portobello or shiitake mushroom powder

1 tablespoon (6 g) chaat masala blend

½ teaspoon ground turmeric

7½ ounces (215 g) dried yellow split peas, soaked in water overnight, drained

½ cup (120 ml) brewed lapsang souchong tea or mushroom-soaking liquid

2 cups (480 ml) water, plus more as needed

2 cups (370 g) cooked quinoa or (400 g) rice

Chopped fresh cilantro or parsley, for garnish

1. In a large skillet over medium-high heat, combine the oil and onion. Cook until the onions start to brown, about 8 minutes, stirring occasionally and adjusting the heat as needed.

2. Lower the heat to medium. Add the miso, garlic, nutritional yeast, mushroom powder, chaat masala, and turmeric. Press down to incorporate the ingredients, making sure the miso gets evenly distributed and has contact with the skillet surface to develop its flavors. Cook for 2 minutes.

3. Add the soaked peas and cook for another minute.

4. Add the tea and water, bring to a boil, reduce the heat, and simmer until the peas are tender, about 30 minutes. Add more water if the peas aren't tender to your liking.

5. Stir the cooked quinoa into the mixture, or serve the stew on top of the quinoa or rice. Garnish with cilantro.

Yield: 4 to 6 servings

PLANET SAVER TIP 27

I often brew extra cups of tea for photo shoots and end up not drinking them because the time of the day isn't right for caffeinated beverages. I cannot bear to throw the tea away so I keep it for my baking or cooking endeavors in the days to come. That's how the lapsang souchong used here came to be. With its deep, smoky flavor, it's a perfect complement to the other savory notes in the stew. Earl grey, jasmine black, green tea, or anything similar would also be good additions.

CHAAT MASALA CHICKPEA POCKETS

Chaat masala is a tart spice mix composed of mango powder (*amchur*), black salt (*kala namak*, often used to mimic the sulfuric taste of eggs in vegan scrambles), mint, and more spices. I love to coat my favorite bean (chickpeas!) with it. Chaat masala can be found at international food markets or online.

FOR CHICKPEAS

1 (25-ounce, or 708 g) can chickpeas, drained, liquid reserved, or 2½ cups (650 g) cooked chickpeas

1 tablespoon (15 ml) roasted pistachio oil, peanut oil, or (14 g) coconut oil

1 tablespoon (6 g) chaat masala

½ teaspoon ground turmeric

¼ teaspoon smoked sea salt or regular sea salt (adjust according to the chaat masala)

FOR TAHINI DRESSING

¼ cup (60 g) tahini

¼ cup (60 ml) water

2 tablespoons (30 g) Cashew Sour Cream (page 95), store-bought vegan sour cream, or plant-based yogurt

2 tablespoons (30 ml) extra-virgin olive oil

2 tablespoons (30 ml) fresh lemon juice

Diamond kosher salt, to taste

1 large garlic clove, peeled

FOR POCKETS

6 pita breads, roti, chapati, or any favorite vegan flatbread, gently heated

Pineapple Tamarind Chutney (page 64), for serving

1 generous cup (200 g) cooked quinoa (see tip, following)

Finely shredded red or green cabbage, for serving

Fresh baby spinach leaves, for serving

Thinly sliced Persian cucumber, for serving

Thinly sliced tomato, for serving

Chopped fresh parsley, mint, cilantro, or a combo, for serving

Dry-roasted pine nuts, pistachios, or walnuts, for serving

1. To make the chickpeas: In a large skillet over medium-high heat, combine all the ingredients. Cook, stirring frequently, until the chickpeas are golden brown and slightly crispy, about 6 minutes. Adjust the heat as needed to prevent burning. Set aside.

2. To make the tahini dressing: In a blender, combine all the ingredients and blend until smooth. Alternatively, combine in a medium-size bowl and use an immersion blender to blend until smooth.

3. To make the pockets: Place one flatbread on a plate. Apply a thin layer of chutney in the center. Top with a couple tablespoons (25 g) of quinoa, a handful of cabbage, spinach, a few slices of cucumber and tomato, a couple spoonfuls of crushed chickpeas, a drizzle of dressing, herbs, and nuts. Serve immediately.

Yield: 6 servings, ⅔ cup (160 g) dressing

PLANET SAVER TIP 28

I love to cook a huge batch of protein-rich quinoa in leftover stale beer or homemade broth to freeze or refrigerate so I have a quick and healthy option for salad or veggie bowls, Herby Quinoa Frittata (page 66), or for a quinoa version of fried rice. It saves on prep time and means you only have to wash that big cooking pot once.

PINEAPPLE TAMARIND CHUTNEY

GF **SF** Perfect as an addition to nut butter sandwiches, baked potatoes, and most Indian-inspired dishes that need an extra kick, this chutney can also be made into a delicious nutty dressing (see Go-To Nut Butter Dressing headnote, page 120).

3 cups (630 g) chopped fresh pineapple

¼ cup (36 g) coconut sugar, (48 g) Sucanat, or (38 g) dark brown sugar

¼ cup (60 ml) distilled vinegar

2 tablespoons (30 ml) rum

2 garlic cloves, minced

1 tablespoon (14 g) coconut oil

1½ teaspoons Diamond kosher salt

1 teaspoon tamarind paste

1 teaspoon onion powder, or 1 small shallot, minced

½ teaspoon ground ginger, or 1 teaspoon grated peeled fresh ginger

1 serrano pepper, trimmed, seeded (if desired) minced

2 tablespoons (19 g) golden raisins

1½ tablespoons (5 g) minced fresh chives

1. In a medium-size saucepan over medium-high heat, combine the pineapple, coconut sugar, vinegar, rum, garlic, oil, salt, tamarind paste, onion powder, and ginger. Bring to a low boil, lower the heat to medium, and cook until thickened, stirring occasionally, 15 to 20 minutes.

2. Stir in the serrano, raisins, and chives. Let cool slightly before transferring to a heat-safe jar.

3. Refrigerate, covered, for up to 1 month. The chutney is best served at room temperature to let the flavors develop.

Yield: 1 pound (454 g)

PLANET SAVER TIP 29

Don't waste the edible blossoms of your homegrown chives. Use them as a lovely decoration on salads and bowls, or make flavored, pink-hued vinegar. Start by removing them from the stem and soaking them in cold water for a good 15 minutes to dislodge impurities and potential bugs. Gently spin them dry, place in a Mason jar, and top with white wine vinegar, or distilled vinegar. You want a good ¼ cup (24 g) of blossoms per pint (480 ml) jar. Cover tightly with a lid and store in a dark place for 1 week. Drain the spent flowers and put the vinegar to good use in your salads.

SRIRACHA BARBECUE SAUCE

I used to purchase a barbecue sauce from Trader Joe's and our love story knew no low notes. I finally decided to try my hand at making my own and the results are simply outstanding, if I do say so myself. I use it to cook my favorite chickpeas (see Barbecue Chickpea Scramble, page 58) and anywhere barbecue sauce is called for. I hope you love it, too!

¾ cup (240 g) agave nectar

½ cup (120 g) organic ketchup

¼ cup (36 g) coconut sugar

¼ cup (80 g) blackstrap molasses

2 tablespoons (30 ml) mirin, rice cooking vinegar, or apple cider vinegar

2 tablespoons (30 ml) vegan sriracha

1 generous teaspoon Diamond kosher salt

1 teaspoon onion powder

1 teaspoon liquid smoke

1 teaspoon vegan Worcestershire sauce

⅛ teaspoon Chinese five-spice powder (optional)

1. In a medium-size saucepan over medium-high heat, combine all the ingredients. Bring to a low boil, lower the heat, and cook until thickened and reduced by about half the original amount, about 30 minutes. Stir frequently and adjust the heat as needed.

2. Let cool slightly before transferring to a heat-safe jar. Refrigerate, covered, for up to 1 month.

Yield: 1¾ cups (18 ounces, or 514 g)

PLANET SAVER TIP 30

Need to use the rest of the barbecue sauce you made? Whip up a batch of Smoky Sausages (page 70) and you'll make a big dent in your stash. You can also easily double the recipe, just bear in mind the cooking time will be slightly longer.

HERBY QUINOA FRITTATA

GF Remember that time you cooked the whole bag of quinoa and froze some for future use? This is where it comes into play. A delicious, nutritious, and filling frittata to be enjoyed by the slice, alongside a big mix of raw and cooked vegetables made into a salad. That's the way I like to eat mine.

Oil spray or vegan butter

2 cups (370 g) packed chilled cooked quinoa

2 tablespoons (40 g) Umami Sofrito (not just the oil, umami mixture included), or 1 tablespoon (15 ml) roasted peanut oil or (14 g) coconut oil

½ cup (120 g) Basil–Carrot Top Pesto (page 109) or pesto of choice

1 cup (240 g) vegan Greek-style yogurt, Cashew Sour Cream (page 95), or store-bought vegan sour cream

1 cup (240 ml) coconut water or vegetable broth (see A Guide to Veggie Broth, page 142)

¼ cup (20 g) nutritional yeast (powder)

1 tablespoon (6 g) broth powder (see Planet Saver Tip 50, page 95)

1 tablespoon (6 g) mushroom powder (if not using sofrito)

2 teaspoons za'atar spice mix

½ teaspoon sea salt, or to taste

½ cup plus 2 tablespoons (75 g) chickpea flour

2 tablespoons (16 g) organic cornstarch

½ teaspoon baking powder

1. Preheat the oven to 375°F (190°C, or gas mark 5). Lightly coat an 8½-inch (22 cm) round baking pan with oil.

2. In a large skillet over medium-high heat, combine the quinoa and sofrito. Cook until fragrant and light golden brown, about 6 minutes. Adjust the heat as needed to prevent burning, and stir occasionally.

3. In the meantime, in a large bowl, whisk to combine the pesto, yogurt, coconut water, nutritional yeast, broth powder, mushroom powder, za'atar, and salt. Once the quinoa is ready, add it to the bowl and stir to combine. Add the chickpea flour, cornstarch, and baking powder. Fold to combine thoroughly. Pour the mixture into the prepared pan.

4. Bake until golden brown and firm to the touch, 30 to 40 minutes: the big difference in estimated baking time is because the moisture of your frittata will depend on the pesto used. If it's on the thicker side, baking time will be shorter. And if it has more liquid, baking time will be slightly longer. Trust the color and firmness cue: the frittata is done when it is golden brown and bounces back when (carefully) poked in the center.

5. Let cool for 10 minutes before slicing, or refrigerate in an airtight container for up to 3 days, or until ready to serve. Reheat leftovers in a 325°F (170°C, or gas mark 3) oven for 10 minutes, or until heated through.

Yield: 6 servings

PLANET SAVER TIP 31

I love using quinoa in this frittata because it brings a fair amount of protein to the mix, but you can use any kind of small seed or grain in its place: millet, buckwheat (which is also fairly rich in protein), teff, amaranth, or couscous all work well. Just like with quinoa, though, use them chilled before sautéing so they get firmer and don't absorb the oil.

YUZU KOJI TEMPEH SANDWICHES

Yuzu kosho is a traditional condiment from Japan, made from yuzu (a tart citrus fruit) zest, ground chile pepper, and salt. Also hailing from Japan, *shio koji* is a funky marinade originating from the fermentation of koji, a cooked grain (usually rice) that is inoculated with the same awesome mold (a.k.a. *Aspergillus oryzae*) responsible for the greatness of miso and soy sauce. These two ingredients combine as a marinade for tempeh, which is then pan-fried and, ultimately, brings its glorious umaminess in sandwich form.

FOR YUZU KOJI TEMPEH
8 ounces (225 g) tempeh, cut into
8 thin slices

2 tablespoons (30 g) shio koji

1 teaspoon red yuzu paste

2 teaspoons toasted sesame oil
or peanut oil

FOR SANDWICHES
8 slices vegan sandwich bread
of choice, or 4 soft vegan
bread rolls

½ cup (120 g) vegan mayo

2 teaspoons toasted sesame oil

Thinly shredded napa cabbage

Pickled cucumber, for serving

Pickled radish, for serving

Pickled carrot, for serving

1. To make the yuzu koji tempeh: Place the tempeh in a shallow bowl. In a small bowl, whisk to combine the shio koji and yuzu paste. Gently apply the paste to all sides of the tempeh, transfer to a silicone reusable bag, and refrigerate to marinate overnight.

2. In a large skillet over medium-high heat, heat the oil. Pan-fry the tempeh slices until golden brown on both sides, about 4 minutes per side. Set aside.

3. To make the sandwiches: Lightly toast the bread.

4. In a small bowl, whisk to combine the mayo and oil. Apply a thin layer on the toasted bread slices. Top with a small handful of cabbage, pickled vegetables, and 2 slices of tempeh per sandwich. Serve immediately.

Yield: 4 sandwiches

PLANET
SAVER TIP
32

If you're anything like me, you love to try new-to-you awesome condiments that sometimes end up looking forlorn in the refrigerator door or pantry. Don't be afraid to get creative with them. It's always better than having to get rid of them. Think of ingredients that are somewhat similar and that you use more frequently (for example, sambal oelek for yuzu kosho, yeast extract spread for soy sauce, shio koji for miso, etc.), and try subbing them for exciting new flavor profiles and less waste.

MAMOU'S FAVORITE MISO BOWLS

When my mom visited us in 2017, she had the bad luck of falling and breaking her hip. Upon her return from a week-long hospital stay after surgery, I made a huge pot of miso soup that she adored, made repeatedly, and mentioned frequently. Here are the guidelines for it.

FOR SRIRACHA TEMPEH

8 ounces (225 g) tempeh, cut into 4 rectangles, each halved to create 2 thin rectangles

2 tablespoons (30 ml) tamari

1 tablespoon (20 g) agave nectar

1 tablespoon (15 ml) vegan sriracha

1 teaspoon ume plum vinegar

1 teaspoon toasted sesame oil

Oil spray

FOR SOUP

2 cups (weight varies, but about 320 g) leftover roasted vegetables of choice (carrot chunks, bell pepper strips, broccoli florets)

1 cup (weight varies, but about 120 g) leftover sautéed greens of choice (bok choy, kale, spinach)

Prepared noodles of choice, for serving (optional)

¼ cup (80 g) white miso, or to taste

2 cups (480 ml) hot water

2 cups (480 ml) mushroom dashi or kombu dashi (see Congee Bowl, page 55) or vegetable broth (see A Guide to Veggie Broth, page 142)

2 large garlic cloves, grated

2 teaspoons grated peeled fresh ginger (optional)

Gochujang or vegan sriracha, for serving (optional)

Toasted sesame oil, for garnish (optional)

Lime wedges, for serving

Chopped scallion, white and green parts, for serving

Chopped fresh cilantro, for serving

1. To make the sriracha tempeh: Place the tempeh rectangles in a 9 × 13-inch (23 × 33 cm) baking dish.

2. In a small bowl, whisk to combine the remaining ingredients, except the oil spray, and pour the glaze onto the tempeh. Brush to apply evenly all over. Refrigerate to marinate for at least 2 hours, brushing again to apply the marinade evenly halfway through the marinating time.

3. Once almost ready to bake, preheat the oven to 375°F (190°C, or gas mark 5). Lightly coat the tempeh with oil spray.

4. Bake for 8 minutes, flip the tempeh, and bake for another 8 minutes until golden brown. Set aside.

5. To make the soup: Have the vegetables, greens, and noodles (if using) heated and ready to eat.

6. In a medium-size bowl, whisk to combine the miso and hot water until fully dissolved. Add the dashi, garlic, and ginger (if using) and whisk to combine.

7. Divide the vegetables and greens among four bowls. Add the noodles (if using). Ladle 1 cup (240 ml) of broth on top. Crumble the tempeh, or slice it thinly, and arrange on top, along with a squirt of gochujang (if using), a light drizzle of sesame oil (if using), a wedge of lime, chopped scallion, and fresh cilantro. Serve immediately.

Yield: 4 servings

What I love about this bowl is that you can use whatever you have handy or feel like eating that day, and it will be ready in no time, regardless. If you don't want to use tempeh, add any kind of tofu, or even soy curls instead. Or use Yuzu Koji Tempeh (see Yuzu Koji Tempeh Sandwiches, page 67). This is where meal prepping comes in handy for evenings when you just want dinner, and you want it *now*.

SMOKY SAUSAGES

These sausages are yet another reason kimchi brine should never be discarded. If you don't have any, use a combination of ⅓ cup (80 ml) vinegar from a jar of Pickled Red Onions (page 115) and ⅓ cup (80 ml) vegetable broth (see A Guide to Veggie Broth, page 142), another homemade kind, or even store-bought broth.

⅔ cup (180 ml) Fennel Kimchi brine (page 117), ginger kombucha, or vegan beer

⅓ cup (80 ml) Sriracha Barbecue Sauce (page 65) or Miso Sake Sauce (page 121)

2 tablespoons (30 ml) liquid smoke

2 tablespoons (30 ml) vegan Worcestershire sauce

2 tablespoons (30 ml) tamari

2 tablespoons (30 ml) toasted sesame oil

1¼ cups (150 g) vital wheat gluten

⅓ cup (27 g) nutritional yeast (powder)

¼ cup (30 g) chickpea flour

2 tablespoons (16 g) organic cornstarch

1 tablespoon (6 g) onion powder

1 tablespoon (6 g) mushroom powder (optional)

1. Have a steamer ready, with its bottom filled with about 2 inches (5 cm) of water, vegetable broth, leftover beer, or a combo of any steaming-friendly liquid you might have in your refrigerator.

2. In a large bowl, whisk to combine the brine, barbecue sauce, liquid smoke, Worcestershire sauce, tamari, and oil. Add the remaining ingredients, including the mushroom powder (if using) and stir to combine thoroughly for 2 minutes. Let stand another 2 minutes while you prepare two large pieces of parchment paper.

3. Divide the dough into 2 equal portions, about 11 ounces (310 g) each. Shape each into a 7-inch (18 cm) log. Place each log at the bottom center of the piece of parchment and roll tightly, twisting the ends to enclose the sausage. Place the sausages, seam-side down, in the steamer, cover, and bring to a low boil. Lower the heat and steam the sausages for 90 minutes. Carefully remove from the steamer and enjoy warm or cooled (as a sandwich meat).

4. Refrigerate in an airtight container for up to 2 weeks. Use as is, or sauté in an oiled pan for uses in sandwiches or other recipes such as Pineapple Fried Rice (page 93) and Smoky Sriracha Tacos (page 90).

Yield: 2 sausages

PLANET SAVER TIP 34

My favorite way to store these sausages once cooled and ready for the refrigerator is to place them in my go-to reusable silicone Stasher storage bags. They don't break the bank and come in a wide array of sizes, shapes, and shades. They're also easy to store, oven-safe, microwave-safe, dishwasher-safe, and can even be used as a sous vide vessel. How's that for efficient? They're also great for marinating tempeh, tofu, or veggies. And since they're freezer-safe, you can use them to store the bananas for your smoothies when the skin is just past the point of safe use and is better off taking a trip to the compost bin.

PULLED JACKFRUIT SANDWICHES

Sweet, savory, and absolutely scrumptious, these sandwiches have earned the coveted "Most-Loved Recipe of the Current Book" title from my significant other, Mister Chaz-arella.

2 tablespoons (30 ml) toasted sesame oil, plus more for serving

2 (20-ounce, or 600 g) cans jackfruit in brine, drained and rinsed, cut lengthwise into strips

1 scant tablespoon (15 g) double-concentrated tomato paste

2 tablespoons (30 ml) tamari

½ cup (120 ml) sweet chili sauce, plus extra for serving

½ cup (120 ml) water

2 heads fermented black garlic, or 3 large garlic cloves, grated

1 teaspoon mushroom powder

1 teaspoon wasabi powder, or to taste

½ teaspoon ground cumin

⅛ teaspoon ground cinnamon

Tahini paste or vegan mayo, for serving

4 soft vegan bread rolls, lightly toasted

Thinly sliced English cucumber, for serving

Chopped scallion, green and white parts, for serving

1. In a large skillet over medium-high heat, combine the oil and jackfruit. Sauté for 5 minutes, stirring occasionally and adjusting the heat as needed.

2. Add the tomato paste and cook until brick red, about 2 minutes, pressing down on it to distribute evenly on the skillet's surface.

3. Add the tamari to deglaze the pan, scraping up any browned bits from the bottom, and cook for another minute.

4. Stir in the sweet chili sauce, water, garlic, and spices to combine. Bring to a boil, lower the heat to a simmer, and cover the skillet. Simmer for 30 minutes, stirring occasionally.

5. Apply tahini on one side of the toasted rolls, mayo on the other (or pick just one for both sides). Place a generous scoop of the pulled jackfruit on top, along with a drizzle of chili sauce and a drizzle sesame oil, if you like, cucumber slices, and chopped scallion. Serve immediately.

Yield: 4 sandwiches

PLANET SAVER TIP 35

Use that sad jar of sambal oelek hiding in your refrigerator to make your own sweet chili sauce. In a small saucepan over medium-high heat, whisk to combine ½ cup (120 ml) rice wine vinegar, ½ cup (120 ml) water, ½ cup (100 g) granulated pure cane sugar , and 2 tablespoons (30 g) sambal oelek. Cook for about 3 minutes to dissolve the sugar. In a small bowl, combine 1 tablespoon (8 g) organic cornstarch and 2 generous tablespoons (35 ml) of the vinegar prep, immediately whisking to combine. Add this slurry back to the saucepan, whisking to combine. Cook until slightly thickened, about 4 minutes. The mixture will become translucent once ready. Let cool and refrigerate in an airtight container for up to 3 weeks. Yield: scant 1¼ cups (275 ml)

MOROCCAN QUINOA VEGGIE BOWL

GF Roasted vegetables on top of protein-rich quinoa and spiced chickpeas, drizzled with a zingy herby dressing, and topped with crunchy toasted nuts: you can't go wrong with that concept. See tips for adaptations.

FOR VEGETABLES

1 large graffiti or regular eggplant, cut into large chunks

1 medium-size zucchini or other green or yellow squash, cut into large chunks

12 pearl onions, or ½ medium-size red onion, cut into small wedges

4 garlic cloves, peeled

2 teaspoons toasted sesame oil

1 tablespoon (20 g) pomegranate molasses

1 tablespoon (15 ml) tamari

FOR BEANS

2½ cups (412.5 g) cooked chickpeas

2 teaspoons toasted sesame oil

1 teaspoon harissa seasoning mix or paste, or to taste

½ teaspoon smoked sea salt or Diamond kosher salt, or to taste

½ teaspoon ground turmeric

FOR GRAIN

2 teaspoons toasted sesame oil or other oil of choice

1¾ cups (324 g) cooked quinoa, chilled

FOR SERVING

Zippy Herb Dressing (page 75), for serving

Microgreens and/or thinly sliced red or green cabbage, for garnish

Pomegranate molasses or lemon wedges, for serving

Pomegranate seeds, for serving (optional)

Fresh parsley and/or mint, for serving

Dry-roasted pine nuts and/or pistachios, for serving

Recipe Continues

PLANET SAVER TIP 36

This recipe is open to any changes you want to make: use whatever vegetable you love the most, changing cooking times accordingly. Don't care for quinoa? Use bulgur, millet, or even couscous in its place. Just make sure the cooked grain is chilled for best pan-frying results. Pick a mix of herbs you have in your garden or in the fridge. Don't want beans? Fry some super-firm tofu or tempeh cubes in a little bit of oil and soy sauce until crispy. It's also easy to make this gluten-free (use tamari instead of soy sauce) provided you purchase certified GF quinoa and nuts. Nix the nuts if allergic and go for seeds if you can have those.

1. To make the vegetables: Preheat the oven to 425°F (220°C, or gas mark 7).

2. Place the veggie chunks, onions, and garlic cloves in a 9 × 13-inch (23 × 33 cm) baking pan. Drizzle with oil, molasses, and tamari.

3. Roast until fork-tender and caramelized, about 24 minutes, flipping once halfway through the roasting time.

4. To make the beans: While the veggies roast, in a large skillet over medium-high heat, combine all the ingredients. Cook, adjusting the heat as needed and stirring occasionally, until the chickpeas are coated, golden, and mostly dry, about 8 minutes. Transfer to a large bowl.

5. To make the grain: Add the oil to the skillet to heat. Add the quinoa and cook until toasted and fragrant, about 4 minutes.

6. To serve: Assemble your dinner bowls or plates by dividing all the components into 4 portions. Drizzle with dressing. Garnish as desired with microgreens or cabbage, extra pomegranate molasses or a squeeze of lemon juice, pomegranate seeds, herbs, and nuts. Serve warm or at room temperature.

Yield: 4 servings

If you cannot find pomegranate molasses, make your own. In a medium-size saucepan over medium to medium-high heat, combine 4 cups (960 ml) unsweetened pomegranate juice with 1 to 2 tablespoons (weight varies) sweetener of choice (I use agave nectar) and 1 to 2 tablespoons (15 to 30 ml) fresh lemon juice. Cook until thickened and molasses-like. Adjust the heat as needed and stir occasionally. This will take a good 1 hour—some things cannot be rushed. The sweetener cuts down the tartness just a touch, while the lemon juice helps the molasses keep a brighter red shade. Set aside to cool before transferring to a heat-safe jar. Refrigerate for up to 1 month.

ZIPPY HERB DRESSING

  FF GF SF Creamy and zesty, this herb dressing is the ideal addition to any salad or veggie bowl, like My Favorite Bowl of Veggies (page 84), and a good way to use a single type or combination of herbs before they wilt on you. Double the recipe for a larger yield. The SF recipe icon applies if using tahini, or a soy-free yogurt.

1 packed cup (weight varies, about 60 g) fresh celeriac leaves, mint leaves, parsley leaves, or cilantro leaves

3 tablespoons (45 ml) fresh lemon juice

3 tablespoons (45 ml) roasted pistachio oil, walnut oil, or extra-virgin olive oil

1 tablespoon (15 g) tahini or plant-based Greek yogurt

1 garlic clove, peeled

Diamond kosher salt, to taste

In a small blender or food processor, combine all the ingredients and process until smooth and blended. Refrigerate in an airtight container for up to 1 week.

Yield: ½ cup (120 ml)

PLANET SAVER TIP 37

The weight of fresh herbs can vary wildly, that's why I usually just grab a big handful as a way to measure, before washing them thoroughly and spinning dry. It's perfectly okay if some of the thin stems come along as they do bring flavor to the plate, and considering they are blended, no stems will get stuck in your teeth.

SICHUAN–FLAVORED MUSHROOMS WITH ROASTED SHISHITO PEPPERS

I used to think Sichuan pepper was too floral for my taste, but the key to loving that wonderful spice is to not be too heavy handed with it. Prepared as a side dish to the mushrooms, the shishito peppers are ready quickly, so work on them while the mushrooms cook so you can serve them simultaneously with fluffy rice of choice.

FOR SHISHITO PEPPERS

8 ounces (225 g) shishito peppers

1 tablespoon (15 ml) toasted sesame oil

Diamond kosher salt, to taste

FOR MUSHROOMS

1½ pounds (681 g) mixed fresh mushrooms of choice (brown, shiitake, king oyster)

1 tablespoon (6 g) mushroom powder

2 teaspoons yeast spread (such as Vegemite or Marmite)

1 tablespoon (15 ml) toasted sesame oil

3 garlic cloves, minced

4 scallions, white and green parts, minced

½ teaspoon ground ginger

1 teaspoon ground red Sichuan peppercorns

1 cup (125 g) dry-roasted peanuts

1 tablespoon (12.5 g) granulated pure cane sugar

1 teaspoon cornstarch

2 tablespoons (30 ml) tamari

1 tablespoon (15 ml) Shaohsing rice cooking wine or dry cooking white wine

1 tablespoon (15 ml) Chinkiang vinegar or rice vinegar

3 tablespoons (45 ml) water

1. To make the shishito peppers: Preheat the broiler. Place the peppers in a large baking pan and drizzle with oil. Broil until blackened, about 8 minutes. Sprinkle with salt to taste and toss to combine.

2. To make the mushrooms: Brush the mushrooms to remove any dirt. Chop them into large bite-size pieces. Place in a large dry skillet over medium-high heat and cook until the mushrooms start releasing their liquid, about 6 minutes. Stir only occasionally. Once the liquid is being released, add the mushroom powder and yeast spread and stir to combine. Cook until the liquid is fully evaporated, about 4 minutes.

3. Add the oil, garlic, and scallions. Cook until softened, about 2 minutes.

4. Add the ginger, peppercorns, and peanuts. Cook for another 2 minutes.

5. In the meantime, in a small bowl, whisk the sugar, cornstarch, and tamari until dissolved. Add the cooking wine, vinegar, and water and whisk. Pour the slurry onto the mushrooms and cook until the sauce thickens, about 4 minutes. Serve with shishito peppers and rice, as desired.

Yield: 4 servings

PLANET SAVER TIP 38

Make it with tempeh if you're not a fan of mushrooms. Cube 8 ounces (225 g) tempeh, trim and chop a red bell pepper, and sauté over medium heat in oil just until golden brown, about 6 minutes. Then carry on from step 3, although the oil will have been added to brown the tempeh. Also note that the yeast spread and mushroom powder used at the beginning of cooking with the mushrooms should be whisked into the tamari mixture instead.

SWEET AND SOUR CARROT TARTE TATIN

A tarte tatin is far simpler to make than its fancy inverted pie outcome would indicate. I made this one with Middle Eastern flavors, because it's impossible to go wrong with such a concept.

FOR FILLING

3 tablespoons (37.5 g) granulated pure cane sugar

1 pound (454 g) drained Pickled Turmeric Carrots (page 114, reserve the brine for other uses)

1½ tablespoons (21 g) vegan butter

2 tablespoons (24 g) Pistachio Dukkah (see Pistachio Dukkah Whole Cauliflower, page 83)

FOR CRUST

1¼ cups (150 g) all-purpose flour

1 teaspoon Diamond kosher salt

Big pinch ground sumac (optional)

2 teaspoons granulated pure cane sugar

2 teaspoons apple cider vinegar

¼ cup (60 ml) roasted pistachio oil or olive oil

¼ cup (60 ml) cold vegan beer or water, or as needed

Pomegranate molasses, for serving

Chopped dry-roasted pistachios, for serving

Chopped fresh parsley leaves, for serving

1. Preheat the oven to 400°F (200°C, or gas mark 6). Line a 9-inch (23 cm) pie pan with parchment paper.

2. To make the filling: Sprinkle the sugar evenly over the bottom of the prepared pie pan. Bake just until caramelized, 5 minutes. Carefully arrange the carrots on top of the sugar, along with the butter, cut into small pieces. Bake for 15 minutes.

3. In the meantime, to make the crust: In a medium-size bowl, whisk to combine the flour, salt, sumac (if using), and sugar. Add the vinegar and oil and stir to distribute the oil throughout the flour, creating little pebbles in the process. Do not overwork the dough. Slowly add the beer and stir just until a dough forms: it shouldn't be too wet, nor too dry. Transfer to a silicone baking mat, form into a disk, and roll into a roughly 10-inch (25 cm) circle.

4. Once the 15 minutes have passed for baking the filling, sprinkle the dukkah evenly on top of the carrots. Carefully apply the rolled-out dough on top of the filling, pushing down on the edges to neaten it.

5. Bake for another 20 minutes, or until golden brown. Let stand for 10 minutes before inverting the tarte out of the pan. This allows the syrup to set and avoid a mess.

6. Drizzle with pomegranate molasses and sprinkle chopped pistachios and parsley on top. Serve with a lightly dressed salad, or sliced summer tomatoes if the season is right.

Yield: 4 servings

PLANET SAVER TIP 39

If pressed for time, use a sheet of vegan puff pastry instead of making your own crust. Baking time should remain the same, just aim for that beautiful golden-brown color. When making the pickled carrots, add a few pieces of fennel frond for extra flavor. Mince them well, because it's unpleasant to get a huge piece of frond stuck in your throat!

SPICY BEAN BURGERS

Nothing quite like indulging in a thick veggie burger! This one is spicy and a wee bit squishy, so you will need a softer kind of bread if you choose to bun it. It could also be eaten in pita bread or wrapped in a tortilla, or simply as is. On the other hand, for firmer results, pulverize corn chips or tortilla chips and add about ¼ to ½ cup (15 to 30 g) to the burger mass. Plenty of room for adaptation here to get the burger of your dreams. Personally, I don't bother with the corn chips or the bun and eat it as is with veggies on the side.

1¼ cups (215 g) cooked black beans, thoroughly patted dry

8 ounces (225 g) shredded sweet potato with skin (from about 1 medium-size sweet potato), thoroughly squeezed and drained

1 cup (80 g) quick cooking oats, plus more as needed

¼ cup (60 g) Cashew Sour Cream (page 95), store-bought vegan sour cream, or vegan mayo

3 tablespoons (15 g) nutritional yeast (powder)

1½ teaspoons taco seasoning

1½ teaspoons porcini or shiitake mushroom powder

1½ teaspoons onion powder

1 to 1½ teaspoons chipotle chile powder, or to taste

½ teaspoon smoked salt, or to taste

Corn chips, finely ground (optional; for firmer patties)

2 tablespoons (30 ml) olive oil, divided

1. In a large bowl, combine the black beans, sweet potato, oats, sour cream, nutritional yeast, taco seasoning, mushroom powder, onion powder, chipotle powder, and salt. Using clean hands, incorporate and combine the ingredients, squeezing lightly to crush but not completely mash them. The mixture should hold together and not be extremely moist: if it is, add more oats as needed, 1 tablespoon (5 g) at a time until firmer. Alternatively, add the corn chips (if using) for firmest results. Use a packed ½ cup (145 g) of the bean mixture to shape into roughly 4-inch (10 cm) patties. Cover and refrigerate for at least 1 hour, up to overnight.

2. In a large skillet over medium heat, heat the oil. Do not overcrowd the pan, so heat 1 tablespoon (15 ml) of oil per 2 patties. Add 2 patties and cook for 6 minutes per side without fiddling with the patties too much, until they are crispy and a dark golden brown. Adjust the heat as needed to prevent burning. Repeat with the remaining oil and patties.

Yield: 4 large patties or 6 small ones

PLANET SAVER TIP 40

I don't know what it is with me and sweet potatoes, but they're the one thing that seems to linger the longest in the vegetable drawer. I fancy eating some, buy them, only to end up not doing anything with them. These burgers are a good way not to waste these poor tubers. If you tend to ignore your poor potatoes, too, keep this recipe in mind as well as the Queso'rprise (page 118), so you'll have a good reason to keep purchasing them—and ignore them no more. There's always a way to use what seems to spend a lifetime in the vegetable drawer. (Provided it's not covered with mold, of course.)

CHILI MAC GRATIN

I love to use leftover pasta cooked in mushroom dashi or vegetable broth for this gratin so everything is packed with flavor and is ready to bake in next to no time. If you are cooking pasta for the sole purpose of making this, note that it doesn't need to be chilled. A 1-pound (454 g) package of pasta will yield the amount needed.

Oil spray or vegan butter

3 cups (weight varies, about 750 g) Mushroom Corn Chip Chili (page 150) or other chili

2 cups (480 g) Queso'rprise (page 118) or other vegan queso, divided

8 cups (1.6 kg) leftover prepared elbow pasta

2 tablespoons (30 ml) roasted peanut or walnut oil, or extra-virgin olive oil

Chopped scallion, white and green parts, for serving

Chopped fresh cilantro, for serving

Lime wedges, for serving

1. Preheat the oven to 400°F (200°C, or gas mark 6). Lightly coat a 9 × 13-inch (23 × 33 cm) baking dish with oil or butter.

2. In a large bowl, fold to combine the chili and 1 cup (240 g) of queso. Fold the pasta into the mixture. Transfer to the prepared baking dish. Top evenly with the remaining 1 cup (240 g) of queso and drizzle the oil on top.

3. Bake for 25 minutes, or until heated through and golden brown on top. Let stand for 10 minutes before serving with chopped scallion, cilantro, and lime wedges for squeezing.

Yield: 8 servings

PLANET SAVER TIP 41

I love to grill corn on the cob in summer and often prepare far more than needed. If the refrigerator is already full to the brim, I just remove the corn from the cob (which I chop up and place in the compost bin), put the corn in a silicone bag, and freeze the leftovers for future use. This is one recipe where such corn would be a welcome addition. Just add 1 cup (175 g) of corn at the same time you fold the pasta into the chili and queso.

PISTACHIO DUKKAH WHOLE CAULIFLOWER

SF Not sure what took me so long to cave and follow the trend of baking a whole cauliflower when I heard nothing but great things about the concept. It's fantastic and fun to cut into once it's ready. Awesome to serve cut up in pita bread with various dips and sauces, such as Labneh (page 127), Cashew Sour Cream (page 95), or your favorite hummus.

1 medium-size head cauliflower, leaves still on

2 tablespoons (20 g) dry-roasted pistachios, finely ground

1 teaspoon harissa spice

1 teaspoon ground sumac

½ teaspoon ground coriander

½ teaspoon smoked sea salt or Diamond kosher salt

½ teaspoon ground turmeric

¼ teaspoon ground cumin

2 tablespoons (30 ml) roasted pistachio or peanut oil

¼ cup (60 ml) sparkling coconut water, beer, or vegetable broth (see A Guide to Veggie Broth, page 142), plus more as needed

1. Preheat the oven to 400°F (200°C, or gas mark 6).

2. Trim the bottom of the cauliflower just so it stands upright when placed in a 9 × 13-inch (23 × 33 cm) baking dish.

3. In a small bowl, stir together the pistachios, harissa, sumac, coriander, salt, turmeric, and cumin. Place 2 tablespoons (12 g) of this mixture in another small bowl and stir in the oil. Store the remaining spice mix in an airtight container at room temperature for use in other recipes, such as the Sweet and Sour Carrot Tarte Tatin (page 78).

4. Pour the coconut water into the bottom of the baking dish, lifting the cauliflower so the water can find its way under it, too. Pour the spice and oil mixture over the cauliflower. Use a brush to make sure the mixture is evenly applied.

5. Bake until fork-tender: the timing will depend on the size and freshness of the cauliflower, 40 to 60 minutes. Use a knife to check for tenderness. Occasionally use the liquid at the bottom of the pan to baste the cauliflower with the brush. If the liquid evaporates, add more water to the pan, using the brush to scrape up any browned bits.

6. Once fork-tender, remove from the oven and let stand just a couple of minutes before slicing and serving.

Yield: 4 servings, 6 tablespoons (36 g) spice mix

PLANET SAVER TIP 42

I used to be flabbergasted at the amount of "waste" the bottom part of cauliflower seemed to yield. You'd pay a certain amount per weight, only to discard about one-third of said weight. How is that fair? It turns out that unless these parts are moldy or otherwise unfit for consumption, they are just as palatable as the florets! It's uncanny the number of things we do out of deeply ingrained habit instead of thinking. (Why am I tossing something that doesn't really look bad in the first place?) Something to ponder when it comes to more than just produce waste.

MY FAVORITE BOWL OF VEGGIES

I can be a bit one-track-minded when it comes to certain meals. I must have a bowl of this every single day, with variations as to which raw and cooked vegetables come into play. I aim for rainbow colors, great textures, and, of course, amazing flavor. Feel free to use fried cubed tofu or tempeh in place of the chickpeas, or any of your favorite plant-based proteins. Avocado and tomato are obviously more than welcome if the season's right! I also love chopped raw yellow beets when they're in good shape. The options are endless.

FOR BARBECUE CHICKPEAS
2 teaspoons toasted sesame oil

2¼ cups (371.25 g) cooked chickpeas

½ teaspoon smoked sea salt, or to taste

½ cup (120 g) Sriracha Barbecue Sauce (page 65)

FOR BOWL
1 cup (weight varies) roasted vegetable of the day (carrot, Brussels sprouts, squash, zucchini, eggplant, Pistachio Dukkah Whole Cauliflower, page 83)

1 cup (70 g) shredded red or green cabbage, or tender salad of choice (radicchio, frisée)

½ cup (55 g) shredded carrot

¾ cup (55 g) chopped raw broccoli or cauliflower

Couple spoonfuls Go-To Nut Butter Dressing (page 120) or Aquafaba Ranch Dressing (page 98), or to taste

Couple spoonfuls Fennel Kimchi (page 117)

Couple spoonfuls Pickled Red Onions (page 115)

Fresh chopped herbs, such as parsley or cilantro, for serving

Toasted nuts and seeds, for serving (optional)

1. To make the barbecue chickpeas: In a large skillet over medium-high heat, combine the oil, chickpeas, salt, and barbecue sauce. Cook until the sauce evaporates, about 6 minutes. Stir occasionally and adjust the heat as needed. Set aside.

2. To make the bowl: Have a large, shallow bowl handy. Place the warm roasted vegetable of choice in one section, add barbecue chickpeas to taste, and place the cabbage, carrot, and broccoli in the remaining sections of that layer. Drizzle with dressing to taste.

3. Top with kimchi and pickled red onions, along with the herbs, nuts, and seeds (if using). Serve immediately, warm, at room temperature, or chilled. (I love this chilled the most.)

Yield: 1 serving, with enough chickpeas for 4 meals

PLANET SAVER TIP 43

I often use the food processor to turn raw broccoli, cauliflower, or carrots into "confetti." The resulting texture and mouthfeel resemble that of eating quinoa or couscous. Try it for a change of pace and texture in your veggie bowl. Just add well-drained, chopped vegetables to the food processor and pulse just until the texture resembles couscous. Do not overprocess and be sure to use well-dried veggies to avoid unwanted moisture and mushiness. It's a handy trick to have with broccoli stems that are a bit tougher to eat in larger pieces. Note that those could also be thinly shaved with a vegetable peeler for more tender results.

SAVORY SWEET CLUCK—FREE STRIPS SANDWICHES

Because I can never say no to a good sandwich. Or to peanut butter. And oh, to Orange-Habanero Jam (page 110). Don't know if you've tried soy curls yet, but if you liked chicken before going vegan, you'll be happy to hear they're the perfect cruelty-free substitute.

FOR STRIPS

8 ounces (225 g) dry soy curls

1¾ cups (420 ml) vegetable broth (see A Guide to Veggie Broth, page 142) or other broth or dashi

¼ cup (60 ml) soy sauce

2 tablespoons (10 g) nutritional yeast (powder)

2 tablespoons (30 ml) vegan sriracha

1 tablespoon (15 ml) toasted sesame oil or any oil

1 tablespoon (20 g) blackstrap molasses

1 teaspoon chipotle chile powder

1 teaspoon ground cumin

1 teaspoon onion powder

FOR SANDWICHES

6 vegan soft bread rolls, lightly toasted

Orange-Habanero Jam (page 110) or vegan hot pepper jelly, for serving

Natural nut butter of choice (lightly salted, dry-roasted cashew, peanut, or almond butter), for serving

1. Preheat the oven to 400°F (200°C, or gas mark 6).

2. To make the strips: In a large baking pan, combine the soy curls and broth. Let stand for 5 minutes, stirring frequently to make sure the curls are soaking in the liquid. Note that the curls won't be fully rehydrated before adding the remaining ingredients. Don't worry.

3. Add the remaining strip ingredients and stir well to combine thoroughly.

4. Bake for 30 minutes, stirring occasionally, until the liquid has been absorbed and the curls are pleasantly browned. Let cool slightly before using in sandwiches. Or refrigerate in an airtight container until ready to use, or for up to 4 days.

5. To make the sandwiches: Spread a generous layer of jam on one side of the toasted bread. Spread a generous layer of nut butter on the other. Pile on a handful of soy strips, close (the sandwich), and open (your mouth). Repeat to make the remaining sandwiches and serve immediately.

6. To reheat leftover strips, place them in a small skillet and reheat on medium heat until warmed through, about 6 minutes, stirring occasionally.

Yield: 6 sandwiches

PLANET SAVER TIP 44

Don't care for bread rolls, but have a ton of flatbreads or tortillas in need of being called for duty? They will work just as well here, just don't call them sandwiches. Go for wraps. Heat them in a skillet for softness with a little bit of char around the edges for extra flavor. Apply the jam on one half of the surface, nut butter on the other. Slap those strips in the middle, and fold. Or roll. Whatever floats your hunger boat.

KIMCHI FRIED "NOODZ"

Who says that rice is the only grain that should get to be fried? My mom used to sauté leftover noodles in oil with shallots and it was one of our favorite treats topped with Fondor (a nutritional yeast–based seasoning). So, the next time you're thinking of cooking a portion of noodles, just throw the whole contents of the package in boiling water and refrigerate what you don't eat for the next day. If you've never had fried noodles before, you're in for a deliciously crispy treat.

2 tablespoons (28 g) coconut oil or (30 ml) peanut oil, divided

2 large garlic cloves, minced

1½ cups (300 g) drained (brine reserved) and chopped Fennel Kimchi (page 117) or store-bought kimchi, gently squeezed dry

3 cups (weight varies, about 600 g) cooked, chilled small pasta or noodles of choice

½ cup (120 ml) kimchi brine, as needed

Sautéed greens of choice

1 pound (454 g) smoked tofu, cubed, and pan-fried

Chopped fresh cilantro, for serving

Chopped scallion, white and green parts, for serving

Dry-roasted peanuts or cashews, for serving

Tamari, for serving

1. In a large skillet or wok over medium-high heat, heat 1 tablespoon (15 ml) of oil. Add the garlic and kimchi and sauté until caramelized, about 5 minutes. Stir occasionally and adjust the heat as needed to prevent burning. Transfer to a medium-size bowl.

2. Wipe the skillet clean and place it back on the heat. Add the remaining 1 tablespoon (15 ml) of oil, along with the pasta. Cook until golden brown and crisp, about 6 minutes, stirring only occasionally and adjusting the heat as needed to prevent burning. Whenever needed, add a few tablespoons of kimchi brine to deglaze the skillet and encourage caramelization.

3. Stir the kimchi into the pasta. Serve immediately with sautéed greens, pan-fried tofu, and preferred toppings. Taste and adjust the seasoning by drizzling with tamari, if needed.

Yield: 4 servings

PLANET SAVER TIP 45

If you don't have smoked tofu or don't care for it, replace it with Barbecue Chickpeas (page 84), Sriracha Tempeh (page 68), or Yuzu Koji Tempeh (see Yuzu Koji Tempeh Sandwiches, page 67). And as far as sautéed greens go, how about using the tougher stems of kale or broccoli that are just as good as their more tender allies, but don't seem to get as much love? They take a little bit longer to cook than wilting greens, but not that much longer. My favorite (and simplest) way to enjoy them is to sauté in oil with minced shallot and garlic, possibly grated peeled fresh ginger, a pinch of salt or a drizzle of tamari.

SLOPPY BULGOGI

All the sloppiness you'd expect, with delicious Korean-inspired flavors.

½ ounce (14 g) dried shiitake mushrooms

1 cup (240 ml) warm water

1 tablespoon (15 ml) toasted sesame oil, or 2 tablespoons (40 g) Umami Sofrito (page 119)

2 large garlic cloves, grated

2 teaspoons grated peeled fresh ginger

1 grated Asian pear or any apple

2 tablespoons (40 g) Gochujang Paste (see Planet Saver Tip 68, page 120), plus more for serving

2½ tablespoons (25 g) sweetener of choice

2½ tablespoons (38 ml) tamari

1½ cups (300 g) cooked lentils

Vegan mayo, for serving

Small vegan buns, halved and lightly toasted

Shredded cabbage (color of choice), Fennel Kimchi (page 117), or store-bought kimchi for serving

Chopped scallions, white and green parts, for serving

Toasted sesame seeds, for serving

1. In a medium-size bowl, combine the mushrooms and enough warm water to cover. Let soak for about 15 minutes until tender. Drain (reserve the soaking liquid for other uses) and squeeze out any extra liquid. Mince the mushrooms.

2. In a large skillet over medium-high heat, combine the oil, garlic, ginger, mushrooms, and Asian pear. Sauté until lightly browned and fragrant, about 4 minutes.

3. Stir in the gochujang to combine. Cook for another 2 minutes. Adjust the heat as needed to prevent burning and stir frequently.

4. In the meantime, in a small bowl, whisk to combine the sweetener and tamari. Set aside.

5. Add the lentils to the skillet and cook for 2 minutes. Add the tamari mixture and cook until saucy yet lightly thickened, about 2 minutes.

6. Serve by applying just enough mayo to cover one side of a halved toasted bun. Spread a thin layer of gochujang paste on the other side. Top with a small handful of shredded cabbage, a generous scoop of bulgogi, a handful of scallions, and sesame seeds. Serve immediately.

Yield: 8 servings

PLANET SAVER TIP 46

Did you know you could regrow scallions? It's true! All you need to do is cut them on the bias right where the light green meets the darker green of the leaves. Then place the bulb, root-side down, in a small, clear glass jar (small enough to keep the scallions from falling, and clear enough to allow for good sun exposure) of cold water and find a sunny location for it. Change the water daily to avoid a slimy mess, which would impede growth. It should take about a week before you can harvest, then consider transplanting the bulbs to a planter filled with fast-draining soil to keep the growing momentum going.

SMOKY SRIRACHA TACOS

It's Taco Tuesday, do you know where your taco is? Don't sweat it: this one's ready quickly and delivers on the flavor front, too!

2 tablespoons (30 ml) toasted sesame oil or peanut oil

1 Smoky Sausage (page 70), minced or crumbled

½ cup (65 g) minced rehydrated dried shiitake mushrooms (soaking liquid reserved for other recipes)

3 large garlic cloves, minced

2 teaspoons grated fresh peeled ginger

1 large shallot, minced

2 tablespoons (30 ml) tamari

1 tablespoon (15 ml) Shaohsing rice cooking wine or dry cooking white wine

1 tablespoon (15 ml) Chinkiang vinegar or rice vinegar

½ small head green cabbage, chopped

6 medium-size flour tortillas, slightly charred while heating

Sriracha Barbecue Sauce (page 65), for serving

Minced fresh chives, for serving

Roasted sesame seeds, for serving

1. In a large skillet or wok over medium-high heat, combine the oil, sausage, mushrooms, garlic, ginger, and shallot. Cook until lightly browned, about 4 minutes. Stir occasionally and adjust the heat as needed to prevent burning.

2. In a small bowl, whisk to combine the tamari, wine, and vinegar. Add it to the skillet to deglaze the pan, scraping up any browned bits from the bottom. Cook for 2 minutes.

3. Add the cabbage and cook until barely fork-tender, or to taste, about 4 minutes.

4. Divide the preparation among 6 tortillas. Drizzle with barbecue sauce and top with chives and sesame seeds. Serve immediately.

Yield: 6 tacos

PLANET SAVER TIP 47

Chinkiang vinegar, a fruity, deeply colored Chinese black vinegar, adds a hint of umami. It can be found at international food markets or online. Chances are it will be cheapest at the food market and way overpriced online. I love its flavor but I also don't want you to run all over the place to find yet another ingredient, so feel free to use rice vinegar in its place. Rice wine vinegar or unseasoned rice vinegar will do the trick. Same goes for Shaohsing rice cooking wine: it's truly awesome if you can find it, but you can replace it with dry cooking wine, dry sherry, mirin, or even sake.

PINEAPPLE FRIED RICE

Let's start with an important reminder: use chilled rice when making fried rice. This ensures it firms up and fries properly instead of becoming mushy and unappealing. If you don't want to use a Smoky Sausage (page 70) in this, use Yuzu Koji Tempeh (see Yuzu Koji Tempeh Sandwiches, page 67) instead, or Sriracha Tempeh (page 68), cut into cubes before sautéing.

3 tablespoons (45 ml) toasted sesame oil or peanut oil, divided

1 large shallot, minced

1 Smoky Sausage (page 70), diced

3 garlic cloves, minced

3 cups (600 g) cooked jasmine rice, chilled overnight

Tamari, for deglazing and serving

1½ cups (315 g) diced fresh pineapple

Roasted or steamed broccoli or other greens, for serving

Vegan sriracha, to taste

Chopped scallions, white and green parts, for serving

Chopped fresh cilantro, for serving

Roasted nuts of choice, for serving (optional)

1. In a large skillet or wok over medium heat, heat 1 tablespoon (15 ml) of oil. Add the shallot and sausage. Sauté until browned all over, about 4 minutes. Add the garlic and cook for another minute. Stir frequently and adjust the heat as needed. Transfer to a medium-size bowl. Wipe the skillet clean if there's any spillage on the side.

2. Return the skillet to the heat and add the remaining 2 tablespoons (30 ml) of oil.

3. Spread the rice in an even layer in the skillet and add a healthy drizzle of tamari to aid caramelization. Cook until golden brown and crisp all over, about 6 minutes. Stir only occasionally and gently break up any large clumps of rice. The rice should smell deliciously nutty once ready.

4. Add the pineapple and cook for another 2 minutes, or until just slightly more tender than raw.

5. Return the sausage to the skillet, gently fold to combine, and serve with broccoli or other sautéed greens, a drizzle of sriracha, extra tamari to taste, if needed, a sprinkle of scallions and cilantro, and a few roasted nuts (if using).

Yield: 4 servings

PLANET SAVER TIP 48

I beg you: do not use canned pineapple. It has none of the taste bud–tingling awesomeness fresh pineapple offers with each bite. Sure, it might be a little more involved prep-wise than simply opening a can, but the slightly larger effort it calls for is so compensated by its flavor. Plus, even an average-size pineapple contains several cups of diced fruit—pricewise, it's most likely more worth it in the end. There are several varieties of pineapple, the most common being yellow-hued. White Jade Pineapple flesh is, as its name indicates, white inside. It is sweeter and less acidic than regular pineapple, which can be a blessing for folks with sensitive digestive systems. It's worth trying, if affordable and available, at least once in your life.

MUHAMMARA

GF **SF** Perfect to eat alongside pita bread with some hummus and crunchy fresh veggies (cucumber, tomato), or even used as a pasta sauce, this dip/spread is ready in no time, especially if you have a jar of ready-roasted peppers in the pantry. Shortcuts can be a good thing. If using as a pasta sauce, the muhammara may need to be thinned with pasta cooking water as it is a bit on the thick side.

2 red, yellow, or orange bell peppers

1 shallot, unpeeled

¾ cup (120 g) roasted walnuts

3 garlic cloves, peeled

2 tablespoons (30 ml) roasted walnut oil or extra-virgin olive oil

2 teaspoons brine from Pickled Turmeric Carrots (page 114) or Pickled Red Onions (page 115) or distilled white vinegar

½ teaspoon smoked paprika

½ teaspoon smoked sea salt, plus more as needed

Freshly ground black pepper, to taste

1. Preheat the broiler.

2. Place the whole bell peppers and unpeeled shallot on a rimmed sheet pan and broil until charred and tender, about 15 minutes. Keep an eye on the shallot to see if it needs to be removed sooner than the peppers. When cool enough to handle, peel the shallot and core the peppers. I personally don't bother peeling the peppers, but it's up to you.

3. Transfer the peppers and shallot to a small food processor or blender and add the remaining ingredients. Process until smooth. Add more brine if the muhammara is too thick. Taste and adjust the seasonings as needed.

4. Refrigerate in an airtight container for up to 3 days.

Yield: 1½ cups (380 g)

PLANET SAVER TIP 49

Bell peppers are part of the dirty dozen that should imperatively be purchased in their organic version. There doesn't seem to be a huge difference in price around here, strangely enough, so it makes it a bit easier to follow the rule. As always, fruits and vegetables that will be fully used should absolutely be organic to prevent the absorption of pesticides. Scrubbing them well with a vegetable brush, one that is especially soft for more tender produce, too, is also necessary. You can make a food-safe cleaning solution to soak produce before use: mix ½ cup (120 ml) apple cider vinegar with 4 cups (960 ml) water, add the produce, shake it around a little, and soak it for a good 5 minutes. Adjust the amount of vinegar and water according to the size of produce to avoid waste. Be sure to rinse thoroughly to wash off the vinegar. The cleaning solution is also good to dislodge any potential bugs from your produce.

CASHEW SOUR CREAM AND LASAGNA SAUCE

GF Ready for use anywhere sour cream is called for, this also makes a great spread on toasted bread. I'm including the recipe used in the Butternut Squash Lasagna (page 96) as it calls for a good amount of sour cream.

FOR CASHEW SOUR CREAM
Scant 2 cups (220 g) raw cashews

½ cup (120 g) unsweetened plain plant-based yogurt

2 tablespoons (30 ml) fresh lemon juice

1 teaspoon Diamond kosher salt

Water, as needed

FOR LASAGNA SAUCE
1 cup (240 ml) mushroom soaking water or vegetable broth (see A Guide to Veggie Broth, page 142)

1 cup (240 g) cashew sour cream

2 large garlic cloves, grated

1½ tablespoons (12 g) organic cornstarch

1 tablespoon (20 g) red miso

1½ teaspoons broth powder (see Planet Saver Tip 50, below)

1 teaspoon onion powder

Juice of ½ large lemon

1½ teaspoons maca powder or nutritional yeast

Few grates fresh nutmeg

1. To make the cashew sour cream: Place the cashews in a medium-size bowl fitted with a lid. Cover with filtered water and give it all a stir. Cover the bowl with the lid and soak overnight at room temperature.

2. The next day, drain and rinse the cashews. Transfer to a high-speed blender with the rest of the ingredients and 2 tablespoons (30 ml) of water. Blend on high until completely smooth. Add more water as needed, 1 tablespoon (15 ml) at a time, but don't let it get too liquid-y. Transfer to a medium-size bowl fitted with a lid and let stand at room temperature overnight so it becomes sour. Once ready, transfer to the refrigerator for another 2 days to allow a slower souring process to develop. After that, the sour cream is ready for use.

3. To make the lasagna sauce: In a medium-size saucepan over medium-high heat, whisk to combine all the ingredients. Bring to a low boil, lower the heat to medium, and cook until slightly thickened, about 6 minutes. Stop cooking the sauce when you can see a trail start to form from the whisk. Set aside until ready to use, whisking again just before use.

Yield: 2⅓ cups (20 ounces, or 560 g) sour cream; about 2 cups (16 ounces, or 480 ml) sauce

PLANET SAVER TIP 50

Make your own broth powder with endless variations. Follow the general idea here and go bonkers with amounts and spice additions of your choice: 1 cup (80 g) nutritional yeast (powder), 1 tablespoon (6 g) mushroom powder, 1 tablespoon (15 g) tomato powder, 1 tablespoon (5 g) onion powder, 1 tablespoon (3 g) dried herb of choice, 1 teaspoon paprika, ground peppercorns and salt to taste (optional). Place all ingredients in a jar fitted with an airtight lid, stir thoroughly, close and give it another shake. Store in the refrigerator, or at room temperature, for up to 1 month. Use 1 tablespoon (8 g) of the mixture per 1 cup (240 ml) for strong-flavored broth, or 1 teaspoon for milder flavor. Yield: about 1¼ cups (113 g)

BUTTERNUT SQUASH LASAGNA

I developed a butternut squash lasagna recipe for another cookbook, a long time ago, and it ended up one of my mom's favorite dishes—so much so that she made it over and over again, be it to impress guests or just for special occasions. I decided to whip up a brand-new version in her honor and I like to think she would have loved this one even more.

FOR SQUASH

1 medium-size butternut squash

1 tablespoon (15 ml) roasted peanut oil or other oil

1 teaspoon Diamond kosher salt

FOR LASAGNA

1 tablespoon (15 ml) roasted peanut oil or other oil

1 cup (130 g) minced rehydrated shiitake mushrooms (soaking liquid reserved)

3 large shallots, chopped

2 tablespoons (40 g) red miso

½ teaspoon smoked sea salt

Generous ½ teaspoon dried rubbed sage

Generous ½ teaspoon chipotle chile powder

Generous ½ teaspoon ground coriander

Few grates fresh nutmeg

4 large garlic cloves, grated

Couple splashes dry cooking wine

2 cups (480 ml) Cashew Sour Cream Lasagna Sauce (page 95)

9 no-boil lasagna sheets

1 cup (240 ml) vegetable broth (see A Guide to Veggie Broth, page 142)

1. To make the squash: Preheat the oven to 425°F (200°C, or gas mark 7).

2. Trim the very top of the squash. Leave the skin on and seeds in. Cut it into large chunks and place them on a large rimmed sheet pan. Drizzle with oil and sprinkle with salt.

3. Roast just until fork-tender (close to al dente, as the squash will continue to bake in the lasagna itself), about 50 minutes. Once cool enough to handle, remove the seeds (discard or keep for toasting), leaving the skin on, if you fancy, and cut the chunks into bite-size pieces. Set aside, or refrigerate until ready to use, if preparing ahead.

4. To make the lasagna: Lower the oven temperature to 375°F (190°C, or gas mark 5).

5. In a large skillet over medium-high heat, combine the oil, mushrooms, and shallots. Sauté until lightly browned, about 5 minutes.

6. Add the miso and press down on it, stirring with the vegetables. Cook for another 2 minutes. Add the salt, sage, chipotle powder, coriander, nutmeg, and garlic. Cook for another minute to release the flavors.

7. Add a couple of splashes of wine to deglaze the pan, stirring well to scrape up the browned bits from the bottom. Stir in the squash to combine and cook for 1 last minute. Set aside.

8. To assemble the lasagna: Evenly spread ½ cup (120 g) of cashew sour cream lasagna sauce over the bottom of a 9 × 13-inch (23 × 33 cm) baking dish. Top with 3 lasagna noodles. Top the noodles with one-third of the vegetable filling. Spread another ½ cup (120 g) of lasagna sauce over the vegetables. Top with another 3 lasagna noodles. Top the noodles with another one-third of the vegetable filling. Spread the vegetables with the remaining ½ cup (120 g) of sauce and top with the remaining vegetable filling. Pour the broth evenly on top. Evenly top with lasagna sauce. Tightly cover with aluminum foil.

9. Bake for 40 minutes. Turn on the broiler. Remove the foil and broil the lasagna for 15 minutes, or until the pasta is tender and the top is golden brown. Let stand for 30 minutes before slicing, as the lasagna will keep its shape better with a little cooling time. Leftovers are the best!

Yield: 8 servings

PLANET SAVER TIP 51

If butternut squash isn't available or you happen to fancy another kind even more, feel free to switch it up. Delicata squash is another favorite of mine with an edible skin I enjoy. Most squashes have edible skins, but it's up to you whether you want to go for it or not. As always, give them a good cleaning and a good scrub before partaking.

AQUAFABA RANCH DRESSING

FF Ranch dressing wasn't something I was familiar with when I first visited the United States. I quickly became fond of it and creating vegan versions is a breeze. You want sourness, onion-y flavor, and richness. Check, check, and check. Pour it on top of your veggies, or dip 'em into it. There's no wrong way to dive in.

⅓ cup (80 ml) aquafaba (drained liquid from a can of chickpeas)

1 teaspoon Diamond kosher salt, plus more as needed for the aquafaba

½ cup (120 g) Cashew Sour Cream (page 95) or store-bought vegan sour cream

½ cup (120 g) vegan mayo

1 garlic clove, grated

1 tablespoon (6 g) packed fresh dill, minced

1 tablespoon (4 g) fresh parsley, minced (optional)

2 teaspoons minced fresh chives

Generous ¼ teaspoon onion powder

Freshly ground black pepper, to taste

1 tablespoon (15 ml) melted refined coconut oil or vegan butter (optional)

1. In a large bowl, using a handheld blender, beat the aquafaba to whip air into it. It will become creamier in both color and texture, doubling in bulk if all goes according to plan. This might vary depending on the brand or sodium content of the one you use. Set aside.

2. In a medium-size bowl, whisk to combine the remaining ingredients, adding blended aquafaba, as needed, until the desired thickness is obtained. Refrigerate in an airtight container overnight before using. If the results are still too thin for what you want, whisk in the coconut oil and refrigerate again for further thickening.

3. Keep refrigerated in an airtight container for up to 4 days.

Yield: 1¼ cups (300 g)

PLANET SAVER TIP 52

We're using chickpea brine, also known as aquafaba, as the slightly-bulky-but-thinning-agent for this dressing. It is beaten into a frothy mixture with the use of a handheld blender. Goya seems to be the brand of canned chickpeas with the aquafaba that works best when beaten into an egg white–like consistency.

ROPA VIEJA TACOS

Ropa vieja (old cloth) is a traditional Cuban dish made with flank steak and served with fresh cilantro, fried plantains, and Cuban-style black beans on top of steamed rice. This version uses the shredded aspect of jackfruit, combined with the sturdiness of protein-rich dark kidney beans.

1 tablespoon (15 ml) roasted peanut oil or olive oil

1 large white onion, diced

1 tablespoon (20 g) yeast spread (Vegemite or Marmite)

1 (20-ounce, or 600 g) can jackfruit in brine, drained and rinsed, cut lengthwise into strips

1 (15-ounce, or 425 g) can dark kidney beans, drained and rinsed

1 red bell pepper, cored and diced

1 serrano pepper, seeded or not, minced

3 large garlic cloves, grated

1½ teaspoons smoked paprika

1½ teaspoons dried Mexican oregano

1½ teaspoons portobello mushroom powder

1 teaspoon ground cumin

½ teaspoon smoked sea salt, or to taste

Freshly ground black pepper, to taste

¼ cup (60 ml) dry cooking wine

1 (15-ounce, or 425 g) can fire-roasted diced tomatoes, undrained

1½ teaspoons distilled white vinegar or brine from Pickled Red Onions (page 115)

Vegan mayo or Aquafaba Ranch Dressing (page 98), for serving

8 medium-size corn tortillas, warmed

Shredded cabbage (color of choice), for serving

Pickled Red Onions (page 115), for serving

Chopped fresh cilantro, for serving

Plantain chips, for serving

1. In a large pot over medium-high heat, combine the oil, onion, and yeast spread. Cook, stirring only occasionally to let caramelize, until browned, about 8 minutes. Adjust the heat as needed.

2. Add the jackfruit, kidney beans, red bell pepper, serrano, garlic, paprika, oregano, mushroom powder, cumin, salt, and pepper. Cook for 2 minutes, stirring occasionally. Add the cooking wine to deglaze the pot, scraping up any browned bits from the bottom. Cook for another minute.

3. Add the tomatoes and their juices and simmer the mixture for 30 minutes until thickened. Stir in the vinegar.

4. Apply mayo on the corn tortillas, or drizzle dressing on top of the ropa vieja prep. Top tortillas with a handful of cabbage, some ropa vieja, pickled onions, cilantro, and chips. Serve immediately.

Yield: 8 servings

PLANET SAVER TIP 53

I love using umami-rich yeast spread to encourage caramelization on vegetables like potatoes, leeks, fennel, onions, mushrooms, and more. Any brand will do the trick here: Vegemite, Marmite, or even Cenovis (hello, Swiss folks). I'm currently partial to Vegemite, which seems to be even more potent than any other brand I've tried. If you've had a jar of the stuff haunting your cupboard since the beginning of time, you'll see it truly is an amazing way to use it.

Pomegranate Ezme
page 132

CHAPTER 4
SIDES

Sides are such a great way to bring variety and extra bulk to a meal, especially when you can finally go back to the good old times when guests popped by unexpectedly around mealtime. I aimed for recipes that are packed with flavor and fun, so boredom has no room in the equation. Because we've had enough of that during confinement, I bet you'll agree.

CRETON

Creton is a pâté originating from Quebec. Traditionally made from ground pork (sadness), it is a distant cousin to France's *rillettes*. The vegan version that follows happens to be the pâté recipe I'm proudest of, with a flavor coming very close to the pâtés I used to eat in my non-vegan days as a youth in Switzerland. Conceited? Usually not, but dang this is good. Try it and see for yourself.

¼ cup (60 ml) liquid refined coconut oil, divided, plus more, melted, for topping

½ large white onion, diced

½ teaspoon freshly cracked rainbow peppercorns, or to taste

2 tablespoons (40 g) white miso paste

2 tablespoons (10 g) nutritional yeast (powder)

1 tablespoon (6 g) portobello or shiitake mushroom powder

1¼ teaspoons ground allspice

2 garlic cloves, grated or pressed

1 cup (215 g) dried split yellow peas, soaked in water overnight, drained

½ cup (120 ml) brewed lapsang souchong tea or mushroom soaking liquid

2 cups (480 ml) water, plus more as needed

½ cup (40 g) quick cooking oats

½ teaspoon smoked sea salt

1. In a large skillet over medium-high heat, heat 2 tablespoons (30 ml) of coconut oil. Add the onion and pepper. Cook until the onion starts to brown, about 8 minutes, stirring occasionally and adjusting the heat as needed.

2. Lower the heat to medium. Stir in the miso, nutritional yeast, mushroom powder, allspice, and garlic. Press down to incorporate the ingredients, making sure the miso gets evenly distributed and has contact with the skillet surface to develop its flavors. Cook for 2 minutes.

3. Add the drained peas and cook for 1 minute.

4. Add the tea and water and bring to a boil. Lower the heat to maintain a simmer and cook until the peas are tender, about 30 minutes. Add more water if the peas aren't tender to your liking.

5. Transfer the mixture to a food processor and add the remaining 2 tablespoons (30 ml) of coconut oil, the oats, and salt. Process until mostly smooth. Transfer to an airtight container and top with a drizzle of melted coconut oil to mimic the usual layer of fat on top of a pâté.

6. Chill before serving on a crusty baguette or in sandwiches. Creton is usually served with mustard. Want a fancier pâté? Follow the en croûte instructions on page 103.

Yield: About 2 pounds (908 g)

PLANET SAVER TIP 54

I buy split peas in a 15-ounce (425 g) bag, so I cooked them all in one shot and used the rest (exactly half, actually) to make Chaat Masala Peas and Quinoa Stew (page 62). Just a heads-up if this is the size of the package you purchase, too. Two birds, one stone. Poor birds.

CRETON EN CROÛTE

What's better than a really, really great pâté on top of a chunk of crusty baguette? A really, really great pâté enclosed in some flaky piecrust.

1¼ cups (150 g) all-purpose flour

1 teaspoon granulated pure cane sugar

1 teaspoon Diamond kosher salt

½ teaspoon freshly cracked rainbow peppercorns, or to taste

¼ cup (60 ml) olive oil

2 teaspoons apple cider vinegar

¼ cup (60 ml) flat vegan lager beer, as needed

2 cups (1 pound, or 454 g) Creton (page 102)

1. Preheat the oven to 375°F (190°C, or gas mark 5). Have a rimmed sheet pan and a silicone baking mat at the ready.

2. In a medium-size bowl, whisk to combine the flour, sugar, salt, and pepper. Add the oil and vinegar and stir to distribute the oil throughout the flour, creating little pebbles in the process. Do not overwork the dough. Slowly add the beer and stir just until a dough forms: it shouldn't be too wet, nor too dry. Transfer the dough to the silicone baking mat and form it into a disk. Roll the dough into a roughly 10 × 6-inch (25 × 15 cm) rectangle.

3. Shape the creton into a roughly 7-inch (18 cm) log and place it in the center of the dough. Fold the dough over the log to enclose it tightly. Cut a few vent holes on top of the pastry. Transfer the silicone baking mat with the pastry onto a baking sheet.

4. Bake for 1 hour, or until golden brown. Let cool for 10 minutes before cutting. Serve with mustard and a nice salad, as desired.

Yield: 4 servings

PLANET SAVER TIP 55

Pressed for time—and you happen to have vegan puff pastry in your freezer? Nix the crust-making action from this recipe but follow the sizing instructions for the log. Fold the puff pastry onto the creton log and bake in a 400°F (200°C, or gas mark 6) oven until beautifully golden brown, about 30 minutes.

SMOKY CARROT SPREAD

SF So very good as a spread on warm pita bread or lavash crackers, served with soups or salads, or to make Smoky Carrot Meatless Balls (page 133). To make your own lavash crackers, it couldn't be simpler: apply a thin layer of oil (I love using roasted walnut or pistachio oil) on the whole surface of the lavash bread, using a food brush. I use the toaster oven for this, putting the bread directly on the racks and just using the toasting option. If using a regular oven, consider putting the bread on a baking sheet to catch the oil if it drips. Preheat the oven to 350°F (180°C, or gas mark 4) and bake just until golden brown all over and crispy, about 5 minutes, but keep an eye on the bread as ovens vary and so does the thickness and freshness of the bread. Break the bread into shards and use immediately.

1 standard bunch carrots with greens attached, about 8 carrots (1 pound, or 454 g), remove and reserve the tops for another recipe

3 tablespoons (45 ml) toasted sesame oil or other oil, divided

Diamond kosher salt, to taste

¼ cup (60 ml) vegan lager beer, brewed lapsang souchong, or vegetable broth (see A Guide to Veggie Broth, page 142), plus more as needed

¼ cup (65 g) roasted almond butter

2 tablespoons (30 ml) fresh lime or lemon juice

1 teaspoon onion powder

1 teaspoon smoked paprika

½ teaspoon chipotle chile powder or Aleppo-style pepper flakes, or to taste

½ teaspoon smoked sea salt, plus more as needed

Fresh parsley, for garnish

Chopped smoked or roasted almonds, for garnish

1. Preheat the oven to 425°F (200°C, or gas mark 7).

2. Do not peel the carrots, but scrub them clean and pat dry. Place them into a 9 × 13-inch (23 × 33 cm) baking dish. Drizzle with 1 tablespoon (15 ml) of oil and a generous pinch of salt.

3. Roast the carrots until fork-tender, about 35 minutes depending on freshness. Transfer to a food processor and add the remaining 2 tablespoons (30 ml) of oil, the beer, almond butter, lime juice, onion powder, paprika, chipotle powder, and sea salt. Process until smooth, adding more liquid, if needed. Transfer to a medium-size serving bowl and garnish with parsley and chopped almonds to serve.

Yield: Generous 1½ cups (14 ounces, or 395 g)

PLANET SAVER TIP 56

Remember to put your oven to good use by roasting several batches of vegetables at the same time. Although it's important not to overcrowd an oven, which can make it less efficient, it's also a waste to have it run full throttle for just one tray of veggies. My oven is average-size and I manage to fit four 9 × 13-inch (23 × 33 cm) baking dishes in there, allowing me to prep ahead for roasted veggie additions to My Favorite Bowl of Veggies (page 84).

NOOCHY SOURDOUGH CRACKERS

Eons ago, I made crackers with nooch, shaped like little ducks, and called them Cheezy Quackers (my husband's idea). We still eat them on the regular but I wanted an updated version that would make good use of the sourdough discard that's invading virtually everyone's fridge these days. This recipe adds that recognizable sour flavor and is even more amazing when stale beer is used as a complement, if extra moisture is needed when making the dough. Double whammy on the no waste part! Actually, make that a triple whammy if you have toasted flour left over from making the roux for Root Veggie Gumbo (page 148).

4 ounces (scant ½ cup, or 113 g) sourdough discard from the fridge

½ cup (60 g) all-purpose or whole-wheat pastry flour (toasted flour leftover from making Root Veggie Gumbo, page 148, is ideal here), plus more as needed

⅓ cup (27 g) nutritional yeast (powder)

¼ cup (56 g) vegan butter or coconut oil

1 teaspoon fine sea salt

Few turns of the peppermill, or to taste

Cold stale vegan lager beer or seltzer water, as needed

1. Preheat the oven to 350°F (180°C, or gas mark 4). Line two baking sheets with silicone baking mats or parchment paper.

2. In the bowl of a stand mixer fitted with the paddle attachment, or in a food processor fitted with the dough attachment, combine the sourdough discard, flour, nutritional yeast, butter, salt, and pepper. Mix or pulse just to combine. Add the beer 1 tablespoon (15 ml) at a time until a dough forms: it should not be too moist or too dry. If it is too moist, add a little more flour, as needed. Avoid overworking the dough.

3. Divide the dough into 3 portions: this will make for an easier time rolling it out and will prevent overhandling the dough. Roll the dough on a silicone baking mat or parchment to a little under ¼ inch (0.6 cm) thick (if using parchment, it can be reused for other baking purposes). Cut out shapes using a small cookie cutter, about 1 to 2 inches (2.5 to 5 cm). Repeat until you run out of dough, rolling it again between batches. Place the crackers on the prepared baking sheets.

4. Bake for 15 to 18 minutes, depending on the thickness, until the crackers are light golden brown on the bottom and quite fragrant. Transfer to a cooling rack. Store leftovers in an airtight container at room temperature for up to 3 days.

Yield: About 45 small crackers, depending on size and shape

PLANET SAVER TIP 57

Nutritional yeast is a gift of the vegan gods. Not really, but you might become addicted to its umami-rich ways and find that purchasing it in bulk is the most clever way to save a few bucks. I store my 5-pound (2.27 kg) bags of the stuff in the freezer or refrigerator to make sure its flavor doesn't get altered when exposed to too much air for too long. Because some brands enrich the "nooch" with vitamin B12, that's another reason refrigeration is key.

OLIVE FENNEL HUMMUS

  Dip those crunchy pita chips in a big bowl of hearty hummus, flavored with brine-y olives and peppery fennel fronds you'll grab straight from the bunch of fennel purchased at the farmers' market! It doesn't get any better than that. Wait, yes it does. Make a fancy Tomato Hummus Soup (page 154) with hummus leftovers. If you want the smoothest hummus, soak and cook your chickpeas with a little bit of baking soda. And peel them before blitzing into a hummus state. (Yes, this is excruciatingly boring and, no, I personally don't bother.)

1 (25-ounce, or 703 g) can chickpeas, drained, liquid reserved, or 2½ cups (412.5 g) cooked chickpeas

½ cup (120 g) runny tahini

¼ cup (60 ml) roasted walnut oil or extra-virgin olive oil

16 dried pitted Kalamata olives

Juice of ½ lemon

1½ teaspoons Diamond kosher salt or to taste

1½ teaspoons Aleppo-style pepper flakes

Big handful fresh fronds from a fennel bulb, chopped

1. In a food processor or blender, combine all the ingredients plus ¼ cup (60 ml) of reserved chickpea liquid. Process or blend until smooth, adding more chickpea liquid as needed, 1 tablespoon (15 ml) at a time, and stopping to scrape the sides with a rubber spatula occasionally, as needed.

2. Place in an airtight container and refrigerate until ready to use. Leftovers can be refrigerated for up to 4 days. Consider adding a thin layer of oil of choice on top of the hummus to prevent it from drying out.

Yield: 2¾ cups plus 1 tablespoon (about 24 ounces, or 675 g)

PLANET SAVER TIP 58

You found fancy-looking fennel at the market, so use the bulb to make Fennel Kimchi (page 117) or vegetable broth (see A Guide to Veggie Broth, page 142)! Any thicker stems can be added to Pickled Red Onions (page 115) for flavor or minced and used in Umami Sofrito (page 119). There's really nothing to toss from our friendly fennel.

BASIL–CARROT TOP PESTO

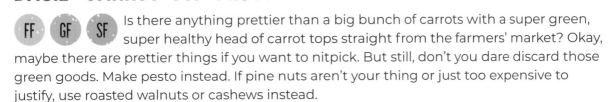

FF **GF** **SF** Is there anything prettier than a big bunch of carrots with a super green, super healthy head of carrot tops straight from the farmers' market? Okay, maybe there are prettier things if you want to nitpick. But still, don't you dare discard those green goods. Make pesto instead. If pine nuts aren't your thing or just too expensive to justify, use roasted walnuts or cashews instead.

1 cup (35 g) loose fresh basil leaves

1 cup (25 g) loose carrot top fronds, stemmed

2 large garlic cloves

½ teaspoon Diamond kosher salt, or to taste

3 tablespoons (26 g) roasted pine nuts (use less for a more liquid pesto)

1 teaspoon maca powder (optional)

Juice of ½ large lemon

¼ cup (60 ml) roasted walnut oil or extra-virgin olive oil, plus more as needed

1. In a small blender or food processor, combine the basil, carrot tops, garlic, salt, pine nuts, maca powder (if using), and lemon juice. Process just until combined, enough for the herbs to be chopped.

2. With the blender running, slowly drizzle in the oil. For a thinner pesto, add more oil as needed. Transfer to a small airtight container and refrigerate for up to 1 week.

Yield: ¾ cup (160 g)

PLANET SAVER TIP 59

I used to discard the top part of carrot bunches until I realized they impart a subtle carrot flavor wherever they are used. Did you know they were accused of being poisonous? Don't run for the hilltops: they aren't. Often likened to parsley, they can taste slightly bitter, so if you want to eat them raw, in salads for example, don't be too heavy-handed with the quantity. Give them a good wash and spin-dry before use, as you do with all leafy greens to lengthen their shelf life and avoid diluting their flavor.

ORANGE—HABANERO JAM

GF **SF** I've always had a soft spot for pepper jelly, and what better way to enjoy something similar in a homemade way. I call this jam because it doesn't have that translucent quality jelly has since the whole fruit is used. You're putting the whole orange to good use here, including the peel, for amazing flavor and color. Be sure to adjust the heat level by choosing to leave the seeds of the habanero pepper in (hot), partially remove them (medium), or remove them completely (mild).

1 medium-size organic orange, scrubbed clean, chopped with peel still on

1 habanero pepper, stemmed, seeded as desired

½ cup (120 ml) unsweetened pineapple juice

½ cup (120 ml) brine from Pickled Red Onions (page 115) or distilled white vinegar

Generous ½ cup (170 g) agave nectar

2 tablespoons (25 g) granulated pure cane sugar

1 teaspoon Diamond kosher salt

1. In a blender or food processor, combine all the ingredients. Blend on high speed until smooth. Transfer to a medium-size saucepan and place over medium-high heat. Bring to a boil, turn the heat to medium, and cook until thickened and reduced by about half the original amount. This will take about 1 hour. Stir occasionally and adjust the heat as needed to prevent burning.

2. Let cool for 10 minutes before transferring to a heat-safe, pint-size jar. Close the jar and refrigerate once completely cooled. Use within 1 month.

Yield: About 1 cup (270 g)

PLANET SAVER TIP 60

There are many recipes where the whole citrus can be used so as not waste a thing and, bonus, maximize flavor. The important thing to keep in mind when doing so is to use organic fruit as non-organic versions are loaded with pesticides and should be peeled before enjoying. Regardless, be sure to scrub the organic fruit with a vegetable brush while cleaning. Remember that although organic fruit is less likely to be covered with pesticides, you still don't know about the cleanliness of the hands that handled it or the places it's been before landing in your fruit bowl.

ORANGE—HABANERO CORN BREAD

SF It's virtually impossible not to enjoy any kind of stew, soup, or chili with a big chunk of crusty bread or corn bread. I packed this version with zesty Orange-Habanero Jam (page 110), flat beer for extra flavor, and a little bit of agave for a hint of sweetness.

Oil spray (optional)

Scant ½ cup (115 g) Orange-Habanero Jam (page 110)

¾ cup plus 2 tablespoons (210 ml) flat vegan lager beer

¼ cup (60 ml) roasted peanut oil or extra-virgin olive oil

1 tablespoon (20 g) agave nectar

1 cup plus 2 scant tablespoons (155 g) white or yellow medium-ground cornmeal

½ cup (60 g) all-purpose flour

2 teaspoons baking powder

1 teaspoon smoked sea salt

1. Preheat the oven to 375°F (190°C, or gas mark 5). Line an 8-inch (20 cm) round or square baking pan with parchment paper, or coat with oil spray.

2. In a large bowl, whisk to combine the jam, beer, oil, and agave. Add the cornmeal, flour, baking powder, and salt and stir just until combined. Pour the batter into the prepared pan.

3. Bake until golden brown on top and a toothpick inserted into the center of the corn bread comes out clean, 26 to 30 minutes. Let cool on a wire rack.

4. Leftovers can be stored in an airtight container at room temperature for up to 2 days, but the corn bread is best enjoyed the day it is baked.

Yield: 6 to 8 servings

PLANET SAVER TIP 61

I plead guilty to using countless cans of nonstick cooking spray in my baking past. They were so convenient, lower in calories, and efficient in preventing sticking disasters that I closed my eyes on the less glorious aspects of such a habit. Not only are they filled with additives, such as soy lecithin, they also contain propellants such as nitric oxide and chlorofluorocarbons, a.k.a. CFC, which is a notorious environmentally *un*friendly propellant. Most brands did away with CFC, but it's best to check the labels thoroughly before buying. Or better yet, put your favorite neutral-flavored oil in a clean spray bottle and use that to coat baking pans.

RED CURRY PEANUT SAUCE

We eat dry-roasted peanuts as a snack on the daily in my household and, therefore, buy them in bulk. The bottoms of the containers are usually littered with smaller bits of peanuts that aren't quite as fun to eat by hand. So, I put them aside and use them to sprinkle on salads or roasted vegetables, in baked goods, or here in this creamy peanut-packed savory sauce. It's great on roasted vegetables, baked potatoes, and pan-fried tofu or tempeh, heated to pour on bowls, or used cold as a dressing—and so much more.

8 ounces (225 g) dry-roasted unsalted peanuts

1 (14-ounce, or 340 ml) can full-fat coconut milk

1 (4-ounce, or 115 g) can vegan red curry paste (my favorite brand is Maesri)

2 tablespoons (18 g) coconut sugar, (24 g) Sucanat, or other brown sugar of choice

2 tablespoons (30 ml) tamari or soy sauce

2 tablespoons (30 ml) fresh lime juice

½ teaspoon tamarind concentrate (optional)

1 black fermented garlic clove or 1 to 2 garlic cloves, peeled

1. In a high-speed blender, combine all the ingredients and process on high speed until smooth, stopping to scrape the sides with a rubber spatula, if needed. Refrigerate in an airtight container for up to 1 week.

2. Reheat the portion you need in a small saucepan on medium-low heat, stirring frequently, until heated through for about 4 minutes.

Yield: A little over 3 cups (750 ml)

PLANET SAVER TIP 62

This recipe calls for two items in steel cans. Did you know these represent the oldest food packaging method, dating back to the fourteenth century? These cans can be recycled endlessly, which means it's important to separate them from regular trash and recycle them properly. The top lid should be removed completely, placed at the bottom of the can, with the can itself pinched closed. This helps prevent animals that rummage through trash from getting their heads trapped in there.

PICKLED TURMERIC CARROTS

  Delicious on their own for snacking or as an addition to sandwiches and wraps, these crunchy carrots also come into play in the Sweet and Sour Carrot Tarte Tatin (page 78).

1 pound (454 g) carrots, tops removed and reserved for another use

⅓ cup (67 g) granulated pure cane sugar

1 tablespoon (11 g) Diamond kosher salt

4 pieces crystallized ginger

1 tablespoon (3 g) whole turmeric tea blend with peppercorn and coconut, or 1 teaspoon grated peeled fresh turmeric with ½ teaspoon whole peppercorns and 1 tablespoon (4 g) unsweetened coconut flakes

2 cups (480 ml) rice wine vinegar or distilled white vinegar, plus more as needed

1. Cut the carrots into thin coins, with a mandoline, knife, or in a food processor. Place in a 1-quart (1 L) Mason jar with a tight-fitting lid. Top with the sugar, salt, ginger, and turmeric tea blend.

2. Pour in just enough vinegar to cover. You might need more or less than noted, depending on the volume of carrots. Stir to combine. Place a piece of cheesecloth on top and loosely tighten the lid. Let ferment for 2 days at room temperature. Refrigerate for at least 1 week before use. Keep refrigerated for up to 1 month.

Yield: 1 (34-ounce, or 1 liter) jar

PLANET SAVER TIP 63

This might sound like a lot of vinegar, but don't freak out: it will not be discarded once the carrots disappear. You can use the now-seasoned vinegar in salad dressings, to deglaze protein, vegetables, and carrots when stir-frying, or anywhere regular vinegar is called for.

PICKLED RED ONIONS

GF **SF** There is a dedicated spot in my fridge for a huge jar of pickled onions. They go well with pretty much everything, except dessert, and are the enemy of bland dishes. Quick to make and ready to enjoy within a day, they also welcome flavor adaptations and the addition of things like hot peppers, peppercorns, or other herbs and spices. I love them in their simplest form: they're anything but boring even then. You could also pickle blanched cauliflower, raw or blanched golden beets, radishes, and pretty much anything you can think of. Versatility at its best.

3 large red onions, halved and thinly sliced

⅓ cup (67 g) granulated pure cane sugar

1 tablespoon (11 g) Diamond kosher salt

1½ to 2¼ cups (360 to 540 ml) unseasoned rice vinegar or distilled vinegar

1. In a 1-quart (960 ml) Mason jar with a tight-fitting lid, place the red onion slices, packing them with a spoon if running out of room.

2. In a medium-size saucepan over medium-high heat, stir together the sugar, salt, and vinegar to combine. Bring to a low boil, lower the heat, and cook for a few minutes just to dissolve the sugar and salt crystals. Turn off the heat and let cool a couple of minutes before carefully pouring the brine into the jar, using a spoon to press down on the onions, making sure they are fully immersed in the brine.

3. Tightly seal the lid and refrigerate for at least 2 hours before serving. Keep refrigerated for up to 2 weeks

Yield: 1 quart (960 ml)

PLANET SAVER TIP 64

Do you usually just compost onion skins? I did, too. Then, I realized they can be cleaned and used to flavor broths, soups, and stews, which I put to the test and found convincing enough to share here. Note that if using red onion skins, whatever you use them in will be pink hued. Having had a lot of issues with rotting-before-their-time onions, I am also going to point out that onions should be firm and dry all over, with thin, papery skins. Onions should also be stored in a dark, dry, and, preferably, cool location. (The latter is laughable if you live where I do.)

FENNEL KIMCHI

Being fairly indifferent to fennel most of my life, imagine my surprise when I realized that kimchi made with fennel is hands-down my absolute favorite version ever. The licorice-like flavor of fennel gets subdued, while the super crunch it offers really shines once fermented. Give it a go if you're usually turned off by its flavor: chances are you'll be pleasantly surprised, too.

2½ pounds (1.13 kg) fennel bulbs (about 2 medium-size, fronds reserved for other uses), thinly sliced lengthwise

3 tablespoons (33 g) Diamond kosher salt (optional)

4 large scallions, white and green parts, chopped

1 apple of choice, thinly sliced

4 garlic cloves, minced or grated

3 tablespoons (24 g) gochugaru (Korean red pepper flakes)

¾ cup plus 2 tablespoons (210 ml) fresh lime juice

½ cup (120 ml) reduced-sodium tamari

2½ teaspoons toasted sesame oil

1. To be honest, I occasionally go rogue and don't always bother soaking the fennel in a salt bath for a few hours before mixing everything. If you prefer doing so to start fermentation and soften the fennel slightly, wash the fennel, cut it into thin strips either with a knife or mandoline, place it in a large bowl with the salt, and stir a bit to combine. Let soak for 4 hours. Thoroughly rinse and drain the fennel.

2. In a very large bowl, combine all the ingredients. Wearing food-safe gloves, massage the ingredients for a few minutes to combine thoroughly. Transfer the fennel and all the brine to a fermentation crock (that's what I use) or a large (1-quart, or 960 ml) Mason jar, pressing down with a clean spoon to pack in the fennel and making sure no air pockets remain. Leave at least 1 inch (2.5 cm) of space at the top of the jar. Loosely seal with a piece of cheesecloth and the lid, if using a Mason jar, and let stand at room temperature for 24 to 48 hours.

3. After 24 hours, open the jar to check for doneness: it should smell pungent and taste sour. Use a clean spoon to press down and release any air bubbles, then replace the lid. Refrigerate now, or if it doesn't seem ready just yet leave it at room temperature for another 12 to 24 hours. Check and press down with a clean spoon again. Your batch of kimchi can be enjoyed now but will benefit tremendously from spending at least another week in the refrigerator. The longer it sits, the more flavor it develops. Use within 1 month.

Yield: 1 quart (960 ml) Mason jar

PLANET SAVER TIP 65

Never, ever toss the brine from any kind of kimchi, be it homemade or store-bought. It's packed with delicious funky flavor and can be used to create the most amazing broths, marinades, and salad dressings. You can even mix a little with mayo to add some oomph to your sandwiches.

QUESO'RPRISE

What's with the name, you ask? The surprise here is that you can use a leftover baked potato from a couple nights ago, roasted cauliflower, or even carrots to add bulk, fiber, and structure to this dreamboat of a queso. Just use roasted vegetables that have a similar flavor profile to the queso concept. Meaning, don't go for Moroccan-flavored veggies to pair with the Mexican flavors queso usually prefers.

1 cup (140 g) raw cashews, soaked in water overnight, drained, and rinsed (soaking optional but recommended)

1 baked russet or other potato, with skin, or roasted cauliflower or roasted carrots (about 8 ounces, or 225 g, roasted potato or vegetables)

1¾ cups (420 ml) vegetable broth (see A Guide to Veggie Broth, page 142) or combination with coconut water from a can

¼ cup (20 g) nutritional yeast (powder)

2 tablespoons (28 g) toasted coconut manna (toasting optional, but recommended; see tip)

1 tablespoon (15 ml) fresh lime juice

½ teaspoon smoked sea salt

½ teaspoon chipotle chile powder

½ teaspoon onion powder

½ teaspoon taco seasoning

½ teaspoon mushroom powder

½ heaping teaspoon maca powder (optional)

In a high-speed blender, combine all the ingredients, including the maca powder (if using). Blend on high speed until smooth and thoroughly combined. Taste and adjust the seasonings, as desired. Serve at room temperature, or gently warmed.

Yield: 3 cups (720 g)

PLANET SAVER TIP 66

The toasted coconut butter (a.k.a. manna) trick was a complete accident. I very nearly burnt my coconut manna one day when trying to liquefy it a bit, as it was quite cold. I was resigned to tossing it but found the smell quite delicious regardless. I decided to try it again in a more controlled and deliberate manner. It's slightly smoky, rich, and perfect to add a little extra flavor and oomph to a recipe. In a small pan over medium-high heat, slowly heat ½ cup (112 g) coconut manna until it darkens a little and takes on a golden brown appearance and smells toasty, stirring frequently and adjusting the heat as needed to prevent burning, about 6 minutes. Let cool before transferring to an airtight jar. Store at room temperature, or in the refrigerator, for up to 1 week. Use on toast, in oatmeal, or hey, hello—in this queso recipe.

UMAMI SOFRITO

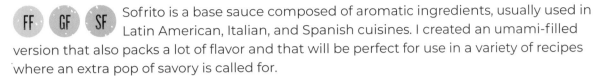

FF **GF** **SF** Sofrito is a base sauce composed of aromatic ingredients, usually used in Latin American, Italian, and Spanish cuisines. I created an umami-filled version that also packs a lot of flavor and that will be perfect for use in a variety of recipes where an extra pop of savory is called for.

½ ounce (14 g) dried mushroom of choice (I use nameko)

Veggie broth (see A Guide to Veggie Broth, page 142), warmed, for soaking the mushrooms

3 garlic cloves, minced

1 medium-size shallot, minced

½ teaspoon Diamond kosher salt, or to taste

¼ cup (60 ml) olive oil

¼ cup (60 ml) roasted peanut oil or other oil of choice

2 tablespoons (weight varies, about 10 g) minced fresh herb of choice (optional)

1. In a small bowl, combine the mushrooms and enough warm broth to cover. Let soak for about 15 minutes until tender. Drain (reserve the broth for another use), squeeze out any extra liquid, and mince the mushrooms.

2. In a large skillet over medium heat, combine the mushrooms, garlic, shallot, salt, and olive oil. Sauté until lightly browned and fragrant, about 6 minutes. Adjust the heat as needed to prevent burning and stir frequently. Transfer to a half-pint (240 ml) Mason jar and add the peanut oil and herb (if using). Note that if you choose a woodsy herb such as rosemary or thyme, add them a couple minutes before the end of cooking time. Cover with a lid and refrigerate for up to 2 weeks.

Yield: 1 half-pint (240 ml)

PLANET SAVER TIP 67

If you don't have shallots around and find that shopping never sounded more unappealing, surely you must have half a red onion somewhere in the house? Or 4 scallions—maybe even ones you've regrown in a jar (see page 89)? A small leek? Any of these can be used instead, the sofrito will be none the wiser.

GO-TO NUT BUTTER DRESSING

This sweet and savory dressing can be adapted to suit your pantry needs. I eat it every day and rarely make it the same way between each prep. It's a win every time! I love to scrape the jar bottoms of various jams and jellies to add as a sweetening agent: quince jelly, orange jam, and apricot jam all work well here. Anything berry would be a little iffy. Get creative and build it according to what you love the most. I also love using Pineapple Tamarind Chutney (page 64) instead of the jam and nix anything else that is spicy.

½ cup (130 g) natural peanut, cashew, or almond butter

½ to ¾ cup (120 to 180 ml) brine from Pickled Red Onions (page 115), seasoned rice vinegar, or 50/50 combo with fresh lime juice, plus more as needed

¼ cup (80 g) quince jelly, or 1 to 2 tablespoons (weight varies) favorite sweetener (agave or Sucanat)

2 tablespoons (40 g) white or red miso (optional, if using gochujang)

2 tablespoons (45 g) chile onion crisp oil with solids, or 1 to 2 tablespoons (20 to 40 g) Gochujang Paste (see tip) combined with 1 tablespoon (15 ml) toasted sesame oil

1 large garlic clove, peeled

Good pinch Diamond kosher salt

1. In a small blender or food processor, combine all the ingredients, including the miso (if using). Process until smooth, adding extra brine if desired, for a thinner dressing.

2. Refrigerate in an airtight container for up to 1 week. If the dressing thickens too much after refrigeration, thin it with lime juice, more vinegar, or even water if you want to keep acidity levels a little more muted.

Yield: about 2 cups (480 ml)

PLANET SAVER TIP 68

Want to make your own gochujang paste? Here's a not-quite-authentic shortcut that will make a big dent in the package of miso you were looking to use before its best-by date.

In a medium-size saucepan over medium-high heat, whisk to combine ½ cup (160 g) white or red miso, ½ cup (160 g) agave nectar, ⅔ cup (160 ml) water or brewed unflavored black or green tea or ginger kombucha, ⅓ cup (40 g) gochugaru (Korean red chile flakes), 1½ teaspoons rice vinegar, 1½ teaspoons toasted sesame oil, and 1 teaspoon onion powder. Bring to a boil, immediately lower the heat to medium, and cook until thickened like tomato paste, whisking frequently as it might bubble, about 15 minutes. Adjust the heat as needed. Let cool. Refrigerate in an airtight jar for up to 1 month.
Yield: 1 cup (320 g)

MISO SAKE SAUCE

I buy large packs of miso and put them straight to work in sauces like gochujang (see Planet Saver Tip 68, page 120) and this umami-filled, deeply flavored brown sauce that's perfect with roasted vegetables, in Smoky Carrot Meatless Balls (page 133), and Smoky Sausage (page 70).

1 cup (320 g) white or red miso

¾ cup (180 ml) mirin

½ cup (160 g) agave nectar

¼ cup (60 ml) sake (I use Gekkeikan regular, found at Target for less than $4)

¼ cup (60 ml) fresh lemon juice

In a small saucepan over medium-high heat, whisk to combine all the ingredients and bring just about to a boil. Immediately adjust the heat to maintain a simmer. Cook for 20 minutes until thickened, like teriyaki (the whisk will start leaving a trail when stirring). Turn off the heat and let cool before transferring to a heat-safe jar with an airtight lid. Refrigerate and use within 1 month.

Yield: About 1½ cups (360 ml)

PLANET SAVER TIP 69

The neighbors' tree loves to drop lemons into our yard. Don't mind if we do—I don't even have to sneakily grab them from the tree! Some houses come with mature trees that new owners or renters might not care about. If your neighbors or friends have trees or berry bushes in their yard and aren't interested in harvesting what grows on them, talk to them about setting the fruit aside for you. If they don't have the time for picking, let them know you'd be willing to help yourself directly. It's a win-win: their yard doesn't get filled with rotten fruit and you get free food out of the deal.

ROASTED POTATO BEER SALAD

My husband has a soft spot for potatoes in all their forms. Baked, fried, in salads, you name it. He can also never resist anything beer flavored. I decide to combine his two favorite things and make him a very happy man, indeed.

FOR ROASTING

1½ pounds (681 g) baby Dutch potatoes, scrubbed clean and unpeeled, halved or quartered to similar size

1 pound (454 g) celeriac, scrubbed clean and peeled

1½ cups (460 ml) vegetable broth (see A Guide to Veggie Broth, page 142)

1 (12-ounce, or 360 ml) bottle vegan beer (stale is fine)

FOR SALAD

½ cup (115 g) vegan mayonnaise, or half mayo, half vegan Greek yogurt

⅓ cup (55 g) minced red onion

¼ cup (60 ml) Zippy Herb Dressing (page 75)

1 garlic clove, grated

Diamond kosher salt and freshly ground black pepper, to taste

Minced fresh celeriac leaves or fresh parsley, for garnish

1. To roast the potatoes and celeriac: Preheat the oven to 425°F (200°C, or gas mark 7).

2. Place the potatoes in a single layer in a 9 × 13-inch (23 × 33 cm) baking dish. Place the celeriac in a single layer a same-size dish. Pour half the broth and half the beer into each dish. Roast the vegetables for about 40 minutes. Reserve ½ to ¾ cup (120 to 180 ml) of the cooking liquid for the dressing.

3. To make the salad: While the vegetables roast, in a large bowl, whisk to combine the mayonnaise, red onion, herb dressing, garlic, and salt and pepper to taste.

4. Add the roasted vegetables, mashing slightly as you combine them with the dressing. Add the reserved cooking liquid, as needed, to obtain a moist salad. Taste and adjust the seasoning. Serve chilled or at room temperature, topped with a generous handful of celeriac leaves.

Yield: 4 servings

PLANET SAVER TIP 70

Don't toss the flavor-packed beer and broth liquid used to roast the vegetables in this recipe. Most of it will be used to thin the dressing, but what's left after that also comes in handy to complement the liquid part of most soups, or to cook rice or other grains. It can also be used as a deglazing agent when sautéing vegetables that become a little too attached to the pan. Just make sure to refrigerate it in an airtight container for up to 1 week.

SPICY GLAZED ROOT VEGGIES

I love root vegetables almost as much as I used to love French fries as a kid. Here, you can use turnips, carrots, or celery root, or anything that strikes your fancy. Just chop them into bite-size pieces and adjust the cooking times as needed. Serve with steamed rice and sautéed greens of choice and your favorite protein. (I love sautéed smoked tofu cubes with this.)

2 tablespoons (30 ml) Umami Sofrito (page 119) oil (just the oil; reserve the sofrito bits) or toasted sesame oil

1 large shallot, chopped

3 large garlic cloves, minced

1½ pounds (681 g) turnips, cut into ½-inch (1.25 cm) dice

3 tablespoons (60 g) Gochujang Paste (see Planet Saver Tip 68, page 120)

2 tablespoons (40 g) agave nectar or other sweetener of choice

3 tablespoons (45 ml) tamari

1 tablespoon (15 ml) unseasoned rice vinegar

1 tablespoon (15 ml) Shaohsing rice wine or dry white cooking wine

1. In a large skillet or wok over medium-high heat, heat the oil. Add the shallot, garlic, and turnips and cook for 6 minutes until the turnips are pleasantly golden brown. Stir occasionally and adjust the heat as needed to prevent burning.

2. In the meantime, in a small bowl, whisk to combine the gochujang, agave, tamari, vinegar, and wine. Add ¼ cup (60 ml) of this glaze to the skillet and cook until the turnips are fork-tender, about 6 minutes. Timing will vary depending on the freshness of the turnips. Add more glaze, as needed, 1 tablespoon (15 ml) at a time.

3. If after this time the turnips are still not fork-tender but you don't want to use the remaining glaze, deglaze the skillet with a little water or mushroom dashi, 1 tablespoon (15 ml) at a time.

4. If you have leftover glaze, refrigerator it in an airtight container for up to 4 days. It can be used to glaze more vegetables, as well as tempeh or tofu.

Yield: 4 servings

PLANET SAVER TIP 71

If the turnips used in this recipe came with a big bunch of greens attached, you are very lucky. They will be perfect sautéed in (sesame, olive, coconut, or peanut) oil with garlic as a side dish to Kimchi Fried "Noodz" (page 88) or Pineapple Fried Rice (page 93) for example. Just wash them well and spin them dry before storing them in the refrigerator, or just before cooking them, for the freshest outcome.

ZA'ATAR CHUTNEY

  This chutney is so zesty and zippy and herby-licious served with any kind of warm flatbread, lentil (and other legume) salads, bowlfuls of pasta or rice, roasted vegetables, and in Herby Quinoa Frittata (page 66)!

1½ cups (105 g) lightly packed fresh parsley

1½ cups (105 g) lightly packed fresh carrot tops

½ cup (120 ml) fresh lemon juice

½ cup (120 ml) extra-virgin olive oil

3 tablespoons (24 g) toasted sesame seeds

2 tablespoons (30 ml) toasted sesame oil

2 tablespoons (18 g) za'atar spice mix, plus more for garnish

2 large garlic cloves, peeled

1 hot green pepper of choice, seeded or not, to taste (optional)

Diamond kosher salt, to taste

In a food processor or high-speed blender, combine all the ingredients and process until combined and mostly smooth. Refrigerate in an airtight container and use within 2 weeks.

Yield: 1 pound (454 g)

PLANET SAVER TIP 72

Feel free to change the herbs in this chutney and use whatever you have on hand, a combination of your favorites, and different oils as well for a different flavor profile. As with many recipes in this book, alterations are more than welcome to use up anything you have to avoid waste.

BEET CRUMBLE

Tangy, sweet, crunchy, and fresh, all in one fell swoop!

1 cup (120 g) light spelt flour

¼ cup (35 g) white cornmeal

¼ cup (28 g) salted dry-roasted pistachios or (36 g) sunflower seeds, coarsely ground

2 tablespoons (18 g) coconut sugar

2 tablespoons (24 g) spice mix from Pistachio Dukkah Whole Cauliflower (page 83) or everything bagel seasoning

¼ cup (60 ml) roasted peanut oil or olive oil, plus 1 tablespoon (15 ml)

Vegan beer, as needed

4 medium-size beets, scrubbed clean, chopped into bite-size pieces

Diamond kosher salt, to taste

Pomegranate molasses, for serving

Mix chopped fresh herbs (mint, parsley), for serving

Labneh (page 127), for serving

1. Preheat the oven to 350°F (180°C, or gas mark 4). Line a rimmed sheet pan with a silicone baking mat.

2. In a medium-size bowl, whisk to combine the flour, cornmeal, pistachios, sugar, and spice mix. Drizzle ¼ cup (60 ml) of oil on top and stir with a fork to combine and create large crumbles. The mixture will be quite dry, and it's okay. Add the beer, 1 tablespoon (15 ml) at a time, stirring to combine with a fork, until the dough is just moist enough to easily hold together when pinched. Do not overmoisten. Crumble the mixture evenly on the prepared sheet pan.

3. Bake for 15 minutes. Using a large spatula, carefully flip the crumbles and bake for another 10 minutes, or until golden brown and crisp. Let cool completely before using. The topping will continue to crisp.

4. In the meantime, increase the oven temperature to 425°F (220°C, or gas mark 7).

5. Place the beets in a 9 × 13-inch (23 × 33 cm) roasting pan, drizzle with the remaining 1 tablespoon (15 ml) of oil, and sprinkle with salt. Roast until fork-tender, about 40 minutes. Let cool to room temperature, or refrigerate, before use.

6. To serve, divide the beets among four plates. Drizzle with pomegranate molasses. Divide the crumble among the four plates and top with a generous handful of herbs. Add a generous dollop of labneh to each plate.

7. Store leftover crumbles in an airtight container at room temperature for up to 3 days. Refrigerate any leftover beets in an airtight container for up to 3 days.

Yield: 4 servings

PLANET SAVER TIP 73

With the sad habit of spraying water on produce to, supposedly, keep it looking fresh, supermarkets end up making said produce spoil faster. Meaning that if I don't purchase beets from the farmers' market, there's just no way I will get to use the tops for anything other than composting. What a waste! Reminiscent of Swiss chard, but a bit sweeter, beet greens can be used just like any quick-cooking greens, such as spinach. Just give them a good wash, spin them dry, and sauté in a bit of oil with garlic and salt. Boom! You've got yourself a great side dish.

LABNEH

A little patience is the only thing needed to create a tangy, thick spread out of plain unsweetened yogurt. Be it homemade, Greek-style, or regular plant-based, the yogurt is strained overnight to rid it of excess moisture. Most commonly used in Middle-Eastern recipes, pair labneh with Pomegranate Ezme (page 132), pita bread, Pistachio Dukkah Whole Cauliflower (page 83), and more.

2 cups (480 g) thick unsweetened plain plant-based yogurt

Pomegranate molasses, for serving (optional)

Pomegranate arils, for serving (optional)

Roasted walnut oil, pistachio oil, or extra-virgin olive oil, for serving (optional)

Za'atar spice mix, for serving (optional)

Green olives, for serving (optional)

1. Line a fine-mesh sieve with a double-thickness of clean cheesecloth. Place the sieve over a bowl. Add the yogurt to the lined sieve and wrap it in the cheesecloth. Twist the cloth or tie it. Cover with a light plate or silicone lid, making sure not to have direct contact with the yogurt to avoid pressing down.

2. Refrigerate overnight (about 8 hours). The longer the straining time, the thicker the yogurt. The yield varies according to the type of yogurt and straining time. Refrigerate in an airtight container for up to 4 days.

3. Serve with garnishes, as desired.

Yield: 1 to 1½ cups (240 to 360 g)

PLANET SAVER TIP 74

Do not discard the resulting liquid that is strained out of the yogurt. It contains yogurt-y good nutrients and can be added to your bowl of oats, salad dressings, or your morning smoothie.

POTATO ROESTI

GF **SF** Roesti are Switzerland's answer to America's hash browns, although I'm not sure who started it first. Traditionally, they can be enriched with cheese, bacon, ham, and anything under the sun. But the best of the best is the unpeeled veggie-friendly option here. Super crispy outside, creamy good inside, and full of flavor. My mom and her brother were both Polish folks born and raised in France who eventually immigrated to Switzerland as adults. They affectionately called these "French fries that stick together." I suppose it's as good a description as any. They're one of my dad's (and now my husband's) favorite things to eat.

1 pound (454 g) Yukon creamer potatoes, unpeeled

1 large shallot, peeled

2 large garlic cloves, peeled

Generous ½ teaspoon smoked sea salt, or to taste

Few grinds freshly cracked black pepper, or to taste

2 tablespoons (28 g) vegan butter or coconut oil

Chopped fresh herbs, for serving

1. Coarsely shred the potatoes, shallot, and garlic. I like to use the food processor for this because 1. I'm lazy and 2. it's noisy but so much faster and my knuckles stay safe. Transfer to a bowl and sprinkle the salt and pepper to taste. Gently fold to combine.

2. In a large nonstick skillet over medium-high heat, heat 1 tablespoon (14 g) of butter. Place the potatoes in an even layer in the skillet in a roughly 8-inch (20 cm) circle. Do not press down. Adjust the heat to medium and cook without fiddling for 15 minutes, adjusting the heat as needed. I like to turn the skillet occasionally to make sure the potatoes cook evenly. You want the bottom to be golden brown and crispy. Once that is accomplished, press down on the sides and surface of the potato disk, pressing into a compact cake. Carefully place a plate on top and flip the skillet to turn the potato cake.

3. Add the remaining 1 tablespoon (14 g) of butter to the skillet and place the potato cake back into the skillet, crisped-side up. Cook for another 15 minutes, or until golden brown and crispy on the bottom.

4. Serve immediately with a mountain of fresh herbs on top and a lightly dressed mix of greens, as desired. My husband likes to enjoy his the American way: with a big glug of ketchup and hot sauce. (Sigh.)

Yield: 2 to 4 servings

PLANET SAVER TIP 75

To keep your potatoes alive and well (so to speak) for the longest time, follow these basic rules: 1. Remove them from any plastic bags, as these don't allow for proper ventilation. 2. Store in a paper bag or basket. 3. Keep in a cool dark place but not in the refrigerator. Potatoes are starchy. The cold turns the starch into sugar. 4. Potatoes that have sprouts but aren't shriveled or moldy are fine to eat. Just remove the sprouting bits and enjoy after a proper scrubbing with a vegetable brush.

SAVORY PICKLE WAFFLES

SF Gotta love it when fennel is sold with glorious panaches of bright green fronds still attached. They can be used in so many ways—minced to top salads, to flavor soups and stews, to make Olive Fennel Hummus (page 108), in crackers, and in this case, blended into zesty and wonderfully crispy waffles. These waffles make a great alternative to regular bread to whip up a good ol' sandwich, too.

¾ cup plus 2 tablespoons (105 g) light spelt flour

¾ teaspoon baking powder

¾ teaspoon Diamond kosher salt

½ teaspoon onion powder (optional)

1 teaspoon granulated pure cane sugar

1 packed tablespoon (10 g) fresh fennel fronds, minced and squeezed dry

3 medium-size dill pickles, minced and squeezed dry

2½ tablespoons (38 ml) roasted walnut oil or other oil

1 tablespoon (15 ml) brine from Pickled Red Onions (page 115) or dill pickles

¾ cup (180 ml) vegan lager beer

1. In a medium-size bowl, whisk to combine the flour, baking powder, salt, onion powder (if using), and sugar.

2. Add the fennel fronds, pickles, oil, brine, and beer and quickly stir just to combine. It's okay if a few lumps remain. Note that the batter will remain somewhat liquid. Cover and let stand for a good 15 minutes.

3. Once the 15 minutes have passed, heat a waffle iron according to the manufacturer's instruction.

4. Use ¼ cup (60 ml) of batter per waffle. Cook until crispy and golden brown, about 6 minutes. Repeat with the remaining batter. You should get 6 waffles. The waffles are crisp from the get-go but, if serving them later, toast before use.

Yield: 6 waffles

PLANET SAVER TIP 76

I've been battling waffle irons for years—all failed miserably, resulting in a waste of money and contribution to landfills. But a $10 machine (Dash Mini Maker) put an end to that battle! This tiny thing has been treating me well for over a year now, despite frequent use. I use ¼ cup (60 ml) of batter in it, and it's the perfect amount for small waffles. Depending on the size of your waffle iron, you might need more and obtain a different yield. Always read your manufacturer's notes to know the quantity of batter you should use for best results.

SOUR CREAM ONION SCONES

If you cannot eat your bowl of soup without some sort of carb-loaded vessel, then these scones are for you. Or, if you have a savory tooth rather than a sweet one for breakfast or brunch, turn to these babies. Richly flavored and terribly cute to boot, they don't take much time to prepare and can be enjoyed warm if you're in a hurry, or at room temperature.

1¼ cups (150 g) all-purpose flour

1 teaspoon baking powder

1 teaspoon Diamond kosher salt

½ teaspoon granulated pure cane sugar

¼ teaspoon freshly ground black pepper

¼ cup (56 g) super cold vegan butter, cubed

⅓ cup (85 g) Cashew Sour Cream (page 95) or store-bought vegan sour cream, divided

3 scallions, white and green parts, chopped and squeezed dry

1. Preheat the oven to 425°F (200°C, or gas mark 7). Line a baking sheet with a silicone baking mat.

2. In a medium-size bowl, whisk to combine the flour, baking powder, salt, sugar, and pepper. Transfer to a food processor. Add the butter cubes and pulse a couple of times to distribute. Add the sour cream and pulse a few times just to form a dough. Add the scallions and pulse just to distribute. Transfer the dough to the baking mat and quickly shape it into an 8 × 4-inch (20 × 10 cm) log. Cut the log into 4 equal scones, leaving a good 1½ inches (4 cm) between the scones.

3. Bake for 22 to 24 minutes until golden brown.

4. Store in an airtight container at room temperature, or in the refrigerator, for up to 2 days. Reheat leftovers in a 325°F (170°C, or gas mark 3) oven for 8 to 10 minutes.

Yield: 4 scones

PLANET SAVER TIP 77

If you prefer using the scallion whites in some recipes without the greens, use only greens in these scones. Or vice versa. Either way, these decadent savory treats are a good opportunity to work through scallions that may not be at their freshest. Minced fresh chives are also a great option.

POMEGRANATE EZME

  This Turkish relish is the best way to enjoy summer vegetables while maximizing flavor and, let's face it, in a stunningly colorful presentation!

2 heirloom tomatoes, finely chopped

Handful cherry tomatoes, finely chopped

2 Persian cucumbers, finely chopped

1 small green bell pepper, cored and minced

1 small red bell pepper, cored and minced

1 mandarin orange, peeled and minced (optional)

½ cup (85 g) pomegranate arils (seeds)

½ cup (50 g) roasted walnut halves

½ large red onion, minced

2 garlic cloves, grated

3 tablespoons (60 g) pomegranate molasses, or to taste

2 tablespoons (30 ml) roasted walnut oil or extra-virgin olive oil

1 tablespoon (9 g) drained capers or handful green olives

1 tablespoon (6 g) za'atar spice mix

Chopped fresh mint, for garnish

Chopped fresh parsley, for garnish

Diamond kosher salt and freshly ground black pepper, to taste

Labneh (page 127), for serving

Pita breads, for serving

In a large bowl, combine all the ingredients, including the mandarin (if using), and gently toss to combine. Let stand for 15 minutes at room temperature to allow the flavors to meld. Serve with labneh and pita bread.

Yield: 4 servings

PLANET SAVER TIP 78

You cannot really go overboard with fresh herbs in this relish-slash-salad, or in any salad. Chop them finely, leaving a few whole as a garnish. If you're reluctant to use the stems, which oftentimes contain almost as much flavor as the leaves, keep them to make pesto (processing them finely), or to flavor broth. The thinner stems are great for enjoying in such a way, while the sturdier stems (think: rosemary, thyme) are best to use for flavoring rather than eating. They're the perfect addition to vegetable broth, even when completely devoid of leaves: the flavor still carries through.

SMOKY CARROT MEATLESS BALLS

The texture of these flavor-packed meatless balls is amazing: tender yet firm. They're the poster child for making great use of leftovers, as they're composed of leftover Beet Crumble (page 126), Smoky Carrot Spread (page 104), and Miso Sake Sauce (page 121).

1 cup (110 g) crumbles from Beet Crumble (page 126)

¼ cup (30 g) vital wheat gluten

Scant ½ cup (113 g) Smoky Carrot Spread (page 104)

¼ cup (60 ml) Miso Sake Sauce (page 121)

2 tablespoons (10 g) nutritional yeast (powder)

1 tablespoon (15 ml) neutral-flavored oil

1 teaspoon onion powder

½ teaspoon Diamond kosher salt

1. Preheat the oven to 375°F (190°C, or gas mark 5). Have a large piece of parchment paper ready, along with a baking sheet.

2. Place the crumbles in a food processor. Pulse until they have the texture of panko bread crumbs. Add the remaining ingredients and pulse until combined. Transfer to the parchment paper and divide into piles of 2½ tablespoons (45 g) of packed dough. Shape into balls. You should get 8 in all. Place the balls on the parchment, fold the parchment over the balls, then fold the ends of the paper to create a packet and tuck them under. Place the packet, seam-side down, on the baking sheet.

3. Bake for 25 minutes until the balls are firm and golden brown. Let cool for 5 minutes before serving. I like to serve them in slightly charred, heated flour tortillas smeared with more Smoky Carrot Spread (page 104) and topped with pickled cabbage and Pickled Red Onions (page 115). They would also be great with Aquafaba Ranch Dressing (page 98) on a bed of shredded cabbage or fresh baby spinach.

Yield: 8 balls

PLANET SAVER TIP 79

I could see adding a small handful of fresh herbs (parsley, cilantro, or mint) to these, but wash the herbs well and spin them dry before use. You don't want too much extra moisture to alter the texture of the balls. Also note that the parchment paper used to steam the balls should be reusable after this recipe, for a new batch of balls or for other savory recipes. Final note: if you don't have Smoky Carrot Spread at the ready but have Muhammara (page 94) or Olive Fennel Hummus (page 108), what a lovely replacement that would be.

Uncanny Chickpeas
page 145

CHAPTER 5
SOUPS AND STEWS

Ah, soups and stews. The poster children for no-waste, extra-delicious comfort food. Packed with veggie scraps a little past their time, these steaming hot bowlfuls are nothing but lifesavers. (Except maybe in summertime when triple-digit temperatures are an everyday occurrence.) Always gaining in flavor and overall awesomeness a few days after preparation, they make such nourishing quick meals paired with crusty bread or crispy crackers.

FINISHING BROWN SAUCE

I see this wowzer of a sauce as a distant cousin to barbecue sauce, but even more so to curry paste: it needs to be added to coconut milk to become the incredible sauce or soup base it was always meant to be. One of its saving graces is that you don't have to worry about chopping things before use as it all goes into the blender once cooked. Laziness for the win!

8 rings (2.5 ounces, or 70 g) dried pineapple

1½ cups (360 ml) unsweetened pineapple juice

½ cup (120 ml) brine from Pickled Red Onions (page 115) or rice vinegar

¼ cup (48 g) Sucanat or (36 g) coconut sugar or (37.5 g) dark brown sugar

¼ cup (40 g) fermented black beans

¼ cup (80 g) agave nectar

¼ cup (60 ml) tamari

¼ cup (40 g) Pickled Red Onions (page 115)

1 teaspoon red pepper flakes

1 head fermented garlic, or 2 large garlic cloves, peeled

2 teaspoons toasted sesame oil

2 tablespoons (34 g) minced crystallized ginger

1. In a medium-size saucepan over medium-high heat, combine all the ingredients. Bring to a boil, lower the heat to medium, and cook, uncovered, for 30 minutes, stirring occasionally and adjusting the heat as needed to prevent burning.

2. Carefully transfer the mixture to a blender and blend until completely smooth and similar in appearance to barbecue sauce. Let cool.

3. Refrigerate in an airtight jar for up to 1 month.

Yield: 2½ cups (600 ml)

PLANET SAVER TIP 80

I love to use dried pineapple in this sauce, the kind that comes sliced super thin and doesn't have sweeteners added. Just like a few other dried ingredients (mushrooms, tomatoes), it packs an even more powerful flavor punch in this application. If it isn't something you can find, use a good ¾ cup (158 g) fresh pineapple chunks instead. I strongly recommend not going with canned, because unlike beans and a handful of other ingredients, some things just weren't meant to be canned. Pineapple is one of them.

EVERYTHING BUT THE KITCHEN SINK LEFTOVER VEGGIES STEW

I love how easy this stew is to whip up. You just add everything to the pot and let it work its own magic. I've used roasted carrots, broccoli, and cauliflower for the vegetables and even a whole head of lettuce that was just a little past its prime. Simply throw it (roughly chopped) in the food processor with a touch of salt and 2 garlic cloves. Adding it at the very end allows it to keep its lovely green hue. The stew itself is packed with flavor from the brown sauce and the simmering action that concentrates its potency even more.

1 (13.5-ounce, or 400 ml) can full-fat coconut milk

1 (15-ounce, or 425 g) can black or brown lentils, undrained (see tip for homecooked)

1 (25-ounce, or 708 g) can chickpeas, undrained (see tip for homecooked)

¾ cup to 1 cup (180 to 240 ml) Finishing Brown Sauce (page 136)

A good 4 cups (weight varies, about 620 g) roasted vegetables of choice, or a mix, cut into bite-size pieces

Fresh chopped cilantro, for garnish

Chopped scallion, white and green parts, for garnish

1. In a large pot over medium-high heat, combine the coconut milk, lentils and their liquid, chickpeas and their liquid, and brown sauce, to taste. Bring to a boil and cook uncovered until thickened to taste, about 45 minutes.

2. Add any leftover roasted veggies you might have. You can also add greens and cook them just until wilted. Top with fresh cilantro and chopped scallion. Serve with crusty bread or your favorite type of flat bread, as desired.

Yield: 6 servings

PLANET SAVER TIP 81

I have become a fervent fan of cooking my own legumes over time, but the convenience of canned goods occasionally comes in handy. Regardless of your preference, know that if you only have homecooked lentils and chickpeas, you will need 1½ cups (300 g) cooked lentils and 2½ cups (412.5 g) cooked chickpeas to replace the cans. You will also need to add 1½ cups (360 ml) vegetable broth (see A Guide to Veggie Broth, page 142) to make up for the liquids from the cans.

KIMCHI—CKPEA STEW

Quick to prepare and loaded with flavor, this one's real comfort food. If you don't have mushroom powder, rehydrate a handful of dried shiitake mushrooms (reserve the soaking liquid), mince them, and add them at the same time as the garlic.

2 teaspoons toasted sesame oil

2 shallots, chopped

2 tablespoons (40 g) white miso

1 cup (240 g) vegan kimchi of choice, chopped

2¼ cups (371 g) cooked chickpeas

3 garlic cloves, minced

1 tablespoon (6 g) shiitake or portobello mushroom powder

1 teaspoon smoked paprika

1 (13.5-ounce, or 400 ml) can full-fat coconut milk

¾ cup plus 1 tablespoon (195 ml) kimchi brine

¾ cup plus 1 tablespoon (195 ml) aquafaba (liquid from a can of chickpeas) or water

1 large bunch fresh kale, stemmed (stems reserved for other uses), or a mix of similar greens of choice, chopped

1. In a large Dutch oven or soup pot over medium heat, combine the oil and shallots. Cook for 2 minutes. Add the miso and press down so it makes contact with the skillet to cook, like you would tomato paste, until fragrant and slightly caramelized, about 4 minutes.

2. Add the kimchi and cook for 2 minutes.

3. Stir in the chickpeas, garlic, mushroom powder, and paprika. Cook for 2 minutes.

4. Stir in the coconut milk, kimchi brine, and aquafaba. Simmer, uncovered, for 30 minutes, stirring occasionally.

5. Add the kale and cook just until wilted. The timing will depend on which greens are used: about 10 minutes for kale leaves or 2 minutes for spinach-like greens. Divide among bowls and serve.

Yield: 4 servings

PLANET SAVER TIP 82

This is yet another recipe that begs for substitutions if they need to be made. If you have bunches of radishes, their greens will be brilliant here. Swiss chard would also be great, but virtually any somewhat-tender greens can be used. Keep in mind some greens wilt faster than others: spinach or bok choy leaves need mere minutes, whereas kale needs a good 10 minutes to become tender. The hard stems that might come along with your bunch should be set aside and sautéed for tofu scrambles, or added to any soup. They could be used here, added with the shallots so they have plenty of cooking time to become tender.

ROASTED ONION SOUP

You've practiced the art of roasting several batches of vegetables together (see Smoky Carrot Spread, page 104) to make the most out of your oven; now the time has come to make soup. So much flavor and very little prep time, now that the oven has done most of the caramelizing legwork.

FOR ONIONS
2 pounds (about 5 medium, or 908 g) red onions, cut into 6 wedges
8 garlic cloves, peeled
2 tablespoons (30 ml) olive oil

FOR SOUP
2 tablespoons (28 g) vegan butter
1½ teaspoons yeast spread (such as Vegemite or Marmite)
2 tablespoons (15 g) toasted flour (see Root Veggie Gumbo, page 148)
1 tablespoon (15 ml) vegan Worcestershire sauce
1½ cups (360 ml) vegan lager beer
2 cups (480 ml) vegetable broth (see A Guide to Veggie Broth, page 142)
4 thyme sprigs
Cashew Sour Cream (page 95) or sliced vegan cheese, for serving
Bread of choice, for serving

1. To roast the onions: Preheat the oven to 425°F (200°C, or gas mark 7).

2. Place all the ingredients in a 9 × 13-inch (23 × 33 cm) baking dish.

3. Roast until caramelized, about 45 minutes.

4. To make the soup: In a large soup pot over medium-high heat, melt the butter. Add the roasted onions and garlic and yeast spread. Cook for 6 minutes to further caramelize the vegetables.

5. Add the toasted flour, tossing the veggies to coat. Cook for another 2 minutes.

6. Add the Worcestershire sauce and cook for 1 minute.

7. Stir in the beer, broth, and thyme. Bring to a boil, lower the heat to maintain a simmer, and cook uncovered for 20 minutes until thickened.

8. Serve with sour cream and bread. If desired, broil each portion in an oven-safe bowl with a slice of vegan cheese on top until melty and golden brown.

Yield: 4 servings

PLANET SAVER TIP 83

Do you have big chunks of artisan-style baguette or other bread that's a little past its prime? Reheat them in a preheated 325°F (170°C, or gas mark 3) oven for about 10 minutes, or until a bit bouncier and crunchier, then dunk them in bowls of this soup, along with the sour cream or melted cheese. They'll have come back to life just in time to make this soup bliss.

A GUIDE TO VEGGIE BROTH

One of the best things you can do to add depth to all those recipes that call for vegetable broth is to make your own. You won't believe what a difference it makes once you simmer and taste your first very own homemade broth. Not only will you be wowed by its amazing flavor, but you will also put to use vegetable parts you would otherwise toss. Whenever you trim vegetables and remove anything that is a bit too tough or less appealing, toss it in a reusable silicone bag and into the freezer for future broth-making uses. You won't regret it.

1 medium-size celery root, scrubbed clean

1 small fennel bulb

10 thyme sprigs

6 rosemary sprigs

4 carrots

1 medium-size leek, rinsed well

4 large garlic cloves, peeled

10 pearl onions, or ½ onion of choice

Diamond kosher salt, to taste

12 rainbow peppercorns

Filtered water

1½ tablespoons (23 ml) extra-virgin olive oil

½ organic lemon

1. In a really large pot or Dutch oven, combine the vegetables and herbs, chopping them into large chunks, if needed, to fit the pot, or leave them whole if they are small enough to fit. The larger they are, the firmer they will remain at the end of cooking time, which will leave them absolutely edible and enjoyable. Choose aromatic vegetables, such as celery and fennel, as well as sturdy herbs such as rosemary and thyme, which will impart their flavors to the broth. Have mushroom stems? Add them for umami! Want a slightly sweeter broth? Dissolve 1 tablespoon (16 g) double-concentrate tomato paste in 2 tablespoons (30 ml) water before adding to the rest of the ingredients. Avoid cruciferous vegetables (cabbage, Brussels sprouts) because the resulting broth might be bitter.

2. Combine with slightly more muted vegetables, such as carrots (to bring a touch of sweetness to balance things) and leek.

3. Add the essentials like garlic, onion, and salt and peppercorns to taste.

4. Add enough water to cover the vegetables by at least 1 inch (2.5 cm). Keep in mind that when bringing the broth to a boil, the levels might rise again, so be cautious not to overfill your pot to keep it from overflowing when your back is turned. Add a healthy drizzle of oil and the lemon half.

5. Cover the pot with a lid, bring to a boil over high heat, then simmer for a good 2 hours, making sure the vegetables stay covered with water and removing any scum that forms around the edges of the water.

6. Strain the broth through a sieve set over a large heatproof bowl, let cool, and refrigerate in an airtight jar for up to 2 weeks. Discard the lemon half

Yield: Will vary, but a 4-quart (3.8 L) pot should yield a good half-gallon (1.9 L)

PLANET
SAVER TIP
84

I personally do not discard the tougher vegetables (celery, carrot, fennel, garlic, and even onion) once the broth is ready and strained, as they are still firm enough to enjoy. If anything turns too mushy or slimy for your taste, discard it.

UNCANNY CHICKPEAS

I readily admit I love the convenience of canned beans. But I had a bad experience with my favorite brand that shall remain unnamed: they sold big cans of beans cooked to perfection, but then something happened and the cans had way more liquid than actual beans. After recurring issues and some very feeble customer service response, I decided to cook my own. I'm grateful because they are even better. And it doesn't even take that long. Not to mention, it's cheaper. In your face, nameless brand.

1 pound (454 g) dried chickpeas, soaked in filtered water overnight

7 cups (1.7 L) filtered water, plus more as needed

3 tablespoons (45 ml) olive oil

Diamond kosher salt, to taste

4 slices dried lemon,
4 slices preserved lemon, or
½ organic lemon

1 fermented black garlic clove, or 3 garlic cloves, smashed

2 thyme sprigs

2 rosemary sprigs

1. Regarding soaking: Pick through the chickpeas. In a large bowl, combine the chickpeas and enough filtered water to cover. Let soak overnight. It can get really hot where I live, so I prefer refrigerating the soaking beans. If it's tolerable where you live, soaking them at room temperature is fine.

2. When ready, drain the beans and give them a quick rinse. Place the beans in a large pot and add the water, oil, a good 2 teaspoons (8 g) of salt, the lemon, garlic, and herbs. Bring to a boil over high heat, lower the heat and simmer, uncovered, until the chickpeas are tender but firm, about 90 minutes. If the liquid evaporates too much, add more water as needed.

3. Drain the cooked chickpeas, but do not discard the broth. Strain it and refrigerate in an airtight container for up to 1 week to use in soups or to cook grains. Refrigerate the cooked beans in an airtight container for up to 1 week. You can also refrigerate the chickpeas in the cooking broth.

Yield: 6 cups (990 g) cooked chickpeas

PLANET SAVER TIP 85

This recipe comes from the concept of cooking vegetable broth (see A Guide to Veggie Broth, page 142). You can add aromatics, if you wish: chunks of celery root, carrot, mushroom powder, onions, or shallots. Whatever's in dire need of being used quickly will do the trick. Also, it may seem unwise to add salt considering it is said to prevent proper cooking of beans, but it turns out we were myth-taken all along. The reason beans are sometimes reluctant to get tender is their age, the water they are cooked in, or even the acidity of the ingredients that might be joining them during cooking.

BABA GHANOUSH SOUP

Baba ghanoush is a Middle Eastern–style dip made of roasted eggplant, tahini, and more flavorful ingredients reminiscent of hummus.

1¼ pounds (567 g) whole graffiti eggplant (about 2 medium)

Generous ¾ cup (195 g) roasted onion purée (see Planet Saver Tip 90, page 153)

¼ cup (60 g) tahini

6 tablespoons (90 ml) vegan lager beer or vegetable broth (see A Guide to Veggie Broth, page 142)

3 garlic cloves, peeled

2 tablespoons (30 ml) toasted sesame oil

1 tablespoon (20 g) red miso

1½ teaspoons harissa spice

1½ teaspoons ground sumac

2 cups (480 ml) water or vegetable broth (see A Guide to Veggie Broth, page 142)

Roasted walnuts, for serving

Pomegranate molasses, for serving

Pomegranate arils, for serving

Fresh cilantro, parsley, mint, celeriac leaves, or other tender herb, for serving

1. Preheat the broiler.

2. Poke the eggplants a few times with a fork and place them on a baking sheet. Broil until super tender, about 35 minutes. Using caution as the eggplants will be hot, carefully trim and discard the woodsy ends only, and transfer the eggplants to a blender.

3. Add the onion purée, tahini, beer, garlic, oil, red miso, harissa spice, sumac, and water. Process until smooth. If using a high-speed blender with a Soup program, that's pretty much all you have to do. If your blender doesn't have that program, gently heat the blended soup in a medium-size pot on medium-high heat for about 6 minutes, stirring occasionally and adjusting the heat as needed.

4. Serve in bowls topped with a handful walnuts, a drizzle of pomegranate molasses, a few pomegranate seeds, and a generous handful of chopped herbs. Enjoy with lavash crackers or pita chips, as desired.

Yield: 4 servings

PLANET SAVER TIP 86

Most commonly, only the pulp of broiled eggplants is put to use in recipes such as baba ghanoush. If that's your preference, it's okay to just scoop out the flesh. Using graffiti eggplant (a purple-and-white–striped variety) means the soup doesn't turn a ghastly unappealing brown color. And even though the skin is charred in some spots due to broiling, there is no bitter flavor.

SUNSET STEW

The combination of coconut oil, peanut butter, and miso lends an almost buttery-cheesy flavor to this hearty healthy stew that makes good use of that big batch of chickpeas you love to make. Also a good way to accompany the simple pan-fried tender greens you want to eat before they go bad!

2 tablespoons (28 g) coconut oil

1 medium-size sweet potato, diced

1 medium-size yellow or white onion, chopped

3 garlic cloves, minced

1 habanero pepper, seeded or not, minced, or quantity to taste

¼ cup (64 g) double-concentrated tomato paste

¼ cup (65 g) natural crunchy or smooth peanut butter or (60 g) tahini

¼ cup (80 g) red miso

1 pound (454 g) cooked chickpeas

1 orange or red bell pepper, chopped

¼ cup (60 ml) Shaohsing rice cooking wine or dry cooking white wine

1¾ cups (420 ml) water or vegetable broth (see A Guide to Veggie Broth, page 142)

Diamond kosher salt, to taste

1. In a large pot over medium-high heat, combine the oil, sweet potato, onion, garlic, and habanero. Cook until the onion softens, about 4 minutes.

2. Add the tomato paste, pressing down on it with a spoon or spatula, and cook until brick red, about 4 minutes.

3. Stir in the peanut butter and miso and cook for 1 minute.

4. Add the chickpeas and red bell pepper. Cook for another minute.

5. Add the wine to deglaze the pot, stirring to scrape up any browned bit from the bottom, then add the water.

6. Partially cover the pot and simmer for 30 minutes, or until the sweet potato is tender, stirring occasionally and adjusting the heat as needed. Taste and season with salt, as needed.

Yield: 4 to 6 servings

PLANET SAVER TIP 87

You're most likely familiar with the concept of portioning leftover tomato paste or chipotle peppers (blended with adobo sauce) from an opened can by the tablespoon into ice cube trays, freezing them, then storing them in a reusable silicone bag until needed. The same applies to curry paste, pesto, or even simple minced fresh herbs. It's a great way to prevent spoilage while creating shortcuts for upcoming cooking sessions.

ROOT VEGGIE GUMBO

This is the tastiest way to use up all the vegetables and herbs I find most frequently in my CSA box to make a comfort food classic, vegan-style.

3 tablespoons (45 ml) olive oil, divided

1 Smoky Sausage (page 70), chopped

¼ cup (60 ml) water

1½ cups (150 g) chopped celery

3 large garlic cloves, minced

1 medium-size yellow onion, chopped

2 tablespoons (32 g) double-concentrated tomato paste

1 medium-size rutabaga, cubed

1 medium-size turnip, cubed

1 medium-size sweet potato, cubed

2 tablespoons (30 ml) vegan Worcestershire sauce

¼ cup (30 g) toasted flour (see tip following)

2 teaspoons Creole seasoning, plus more as needed

2 teaspoons mushroom powder

1 green or red bell pepper, cored and chopped

4 cups (960 ml) vegetable broth (see A Guide to Veggie Broth, page 142)

Diamond kosher salt and freshly ground black pepper, to taste

Chopped fresh parsley, for garnish

Orange-Habanero Corn Bread (page 112), for serving

1. In a large pot over medium heat, heat 1½ tablespoons (23 ml) of oil. Add the sausage and sauté until brown, about 4 minutes. Remove the sausage. Add the water to the pot to deglaze it, stirring to scrap up any browned bits from the bottom, and transfer the water to a glass measuring cup. Set aside.

2. Add the remaining 1½ tablespoons (23 ml) of oil to the pot. Increase the heat to medium-high and add the celery, garlic, and onion. Sauté until softened, about 2 minutes. Add the tomato paste, rutabaga, turnip, and sweet potato. Sauté for 8 minutes.

3. In the meantime, prepare the roux: add enough water to the glass measuring cup that contains the deglazing water to reach the ½-cup (120 ml) mark. Stir in the Worcestershire sauce. Place the flour in a medium-size bowl. Slowly whisk the Worcestershire mixture into the flour, making sure to get rid of all the lumps. Set aside.

4. Add the Creole seasoning, mushroom powder, and red bell pepper to the pot of vegetables. Cook for 2 minutes.

5. Pour the roux over the vegetables, along with the broth. Partially cover the pot and simmer for 30 minutes, stirring occasionally. Remove the lid and cook for another 30 minutes, or until thickened and the vegetables are fork-tender. Have a taste and season with salt and pepper, if needed. Ideally, serve reheated the next day for tastiest results. Top with fresh parsley and serve with a big chunk of corn bread, possibly slathered with vegan butter, if that's your thing.

Yield: 8 servings

PLANET SAVER TIP 88

Don't throw away the rest of the toasted flour. You will have ¼ cup (30 g) left after making the gumbo. It can be used in the Noochy Sourdough Crackers (page 107), or to make this gumbo again because it's so good you won't be able to stop yourself. To toast the flour, place ½ cup (60 g) all-purpose flour in a 9 × 13-inch (23 × 33 cm) baking pan. Place in a preheated 350°F (180°C, or gas mark 4) oven and bake until deep golden brown, tossing frequently, for about 45 minutes. Check often to prevent burning. Let cool. Store in a silicone bag at room temperature, or in the refrigerator.

MUSHROOM CORN CHIP CHILI

Hate reaching the bottom of the bag of corn or tortilla chips where what remains is crushed or stale or has seen too many hungry hands not to feel unappealing by now? Me, too. Adding them to your big pot of chili means a thicker outcome, with an extra layer or corn-y goodness. You think such a small amount of chips won't make a difference to the chili? I assure you, it does.

1½ pounds (681 g) cremini mushrooms, brushed clean, halved, quartered, or minced, or to taste

2 shallots, minced

1 tablespoon (20 g) yeast spread (such as Vegemite or Marmite)

2 tablespoons (40 g) Umami Sofrito (page 119)

1 tablespoon (8 g) broth powder (see Planet Saver Tip 50, page 95; adjust as needed)

1½ teaspoons taco seasoning

1½ teaspoons chipotle chile powder, or to taste

½ teaspoon smoked sea salt, or to taste

½ teaspoon ground cumin

1 (15-ounce, or 425 g) can kidney beans with liquid

1 (15-ounce, or 425 g) can black beans with liquid

1 (28-ounce, or 794 g) can fire-roasted crushed tomatoes, undrained

⅓ cup (20 g) corn chips (such as Fritos), plus more for serving

Queso'rprise (page 118), for serving

Lime wedges, for serving

1. In a large saucepan over medium-high heat, combine the mushrooms and shallots. Cook until the mushrooms release their liquid: the timing will depend on how you chose to chop your mushrooms. Up to 20 minutes if left whole, less time if smaller. Once the liquid is well underway being released, add the yeast spread and stir to combine. Cook until the liquid has completely evaporated and the mushrooms caramelize, about 6 minutes. Stir often and adjust the heat as needed.

2. Add the sofrito, broth powder, taco seasoning, chipotle powder, salt, and cumin. Cook just to toast the spices, 1 minute.

3. Add the beans and their liquid and the tomatoes and their juice. Increase the heat and cook until the chili starts to bubble. Add the corn chips and lower the heat to a simmer. Simmer, uncovered, until thickened, about 30 minutes.

4. Serve with queso, more corn chips, and lime wedges. Cooled leftovers can be refrigerated in an airtight container for up to 4 days. Consider making Chili Mac Gratin (page 82) with them, if you fancy!

Yield: 6 to 8 servings

PLANET SAVER TIP 89

If you prefer fresh tomatoes and home-cooked beans, keep in mind that one 15-ounce (425 g) can of beans usually yields 1½ cups (weight varies) of the goods. As far as the liquid that's called for here, simply add ½ cup (120 ml) water per can to the preparation (so 1 cup, or 240 ml total for the beans), and you'll be golden. If using fresh tomatoes, don't worry about adding extra water for the juices. The fruit (yes, it's a fruit) will have enough on the inside to make up for the difference. So, go for the same weight of fresh tomatoes.

CARROT TOP–PEA SOUP WITH PESTO

  Kinda fancy-looking while super quick to make, this herb-y soup is the perfect complement to the sourdough loaf you got into baking when the world got hit by a pandemic. Which is, hopefully, but a bad memory by the time you read this. Fingers crossed.

1 (13.5-ounce, or 400 ml) can full-fat coconut milk

1 cup (240 ml) vegetable broth (see A Guide to Veggie Broth, page 142)

1 tablespoon (20 g) roasted onion purée (see tip, following), plus more for serving

1 teaspoon Diamond kosher salt, or to taste

1 to 2 garlic cloves, grated

¼ teaspoon ground ginger

1 pound (454 g) frozen petite green peas, thawed and drained

Basil–Carrot Top Pesto (page 109), for serving

Fresh basil leaves, for garnish

1. In a large pot over medium-high heat, bring the coconut milk and broth to a boil. Lower the heat to maintain a simmer and cook, uncovered, for a couple of minutes.

2. Add the onion purée, salt, garlic, ginger, and peas. Simmer just to warm the peas, about 3 minutes. They must remain bright green and with a firm consistency for best results.

3. At this point, you are free to either partially blend the soup or leave it as is. If you want to blend it, remove a few ladles of peas before blending to keep some texture going. Add pesto to taste.

4. Garnish each portion with a little more pesto, onion purée, and a few small basil leaves.

Yield: 4 servings

PLANET SAVER TIP 90

Turn white onions into a creamy, mellow, sweet mixture that will take your soups to another flavor dimension while making them look good, too. Gently scrub as many unpeeled onions as you wish and pat them dry. Preheat the oven to 425°F (220°C, or gas mark 7). Place the onions on a rimmed sheet pan. Roast until the onions are super tender, about 1 hour. Wait a bit for the onions to cool. Once they can be handled without burning your hands, remove the peels and place the onions in a food processor or blender. Blend until completely smooth. Refrigerate in an airtight container for up to 1 week. Yield will vary, but 1 large onion usually yields 1 cup (240 g).

TOMATO HUMMUS SOUP

Did you know that tomatoes impart umami to your dishes, whether used raw, dried, or cooked? If you need proof, wait until you have a bowlful of this soup, with a good helping of hummus stirred into it for extra flavor, protein, and creaminess.

2 tablespoons (40 g) Umami Sofrito (page 119)

¼ cup (15 g) minced fennel ribs and fronds

1 shallot, minced

3 garlic cloves, minced

1 tablespoon (16 g) double-concentrated tomato paste

2 teaspoons smoked paprika

1 tablespoon (15 g) tomato powder (optional)

1 tablespoon (6 g) porcini or other mushroom powder

2 teaspoons Aleppo-style pepper flakes, or to taste

Splash aged balsamic vinegar, to deglaze

1 (28-ounce, or 794 g) can fire-roasted crushed tomatoes, undrained

1 heaping cup (270 g) Olive Fennel Hummus (page 108)

Diamond kosher salt and freshly ground black pepper, to taste

1. In a large saucepan over medium heat, heat the sofrito. Add the fennel, shallot, garlic, and tomato paste. Cook until fragrant and the paste is brick red, about 4 minutes, stirring frequently and adjusting the heat as needed to prevent burning.

2. Stir in the paprika, tomato powder (if using), mushroom powder, and pepper flakes. Cook for 1 minute. Deglaze the pan with a splash of vinegar, stirring to loosen any browned bits on the bottom.

3. Add the tomatoes and their juice. Fill the can with water and add it to the saucepan, stirring well to combine.

4. Stir in the hummus. Simmer the soup, uncovered, for 30 minutes, stirring occasionally. Taste and season with salt and pepper, as needed.

5. Garnish with a dollop of vegan Greek-style yogurt, a few pan-fried chickpeas (in oil with salt and Aleppo-style pepper flakes or regular pepper), and a sprinkling of chopped fennel fronds, as you like. Serve with pita chips and olives of choice, if desired.

Yield: 4 to 6 servings

PLANET SAVER TIP 91

If you have a garden or have access to fresh tomatoes that look a bit past their prime, they will be great to use instead of the canned ones here. You will need the same amount of tomatoes, possibly having to add a little extra water if the soup is too thick for your taste. Looking for that same fire-roasted flavor the can provides? Simply add a few drops of liquid smoke to the soup. It's magic!

Any Fruit
Frangipane Galette
page 169

CHAPTER 6
DESSERTS AND SNACKS

You've reached the end of the meal, yet still have room for a little something-something to take the edge off that lingering hunger, or possibly make a bad day a little more bearable? This chapter's mission is to solve either of these issues, while attempting to reduce waste of any kind in your kitchen—be it by making the most of every single part of seasonal fruit, using the rest of the nut butter jar, or getting the last drop from the bottle of plant-based milk or kombucha.
No waste, just perfectly great taste.

CITRUS QUARK–ALIKE CAKE

SF Quark is a type of fresh cheese, similar to *fromage frais* or queso fresco. Quark cake is a crustless, more cake-like version of cheesecake. When I was a teenager, my mom and I had this ritual of purchasing a big slice of scrumptious lemon-flavored quark cake from the local cheese shop. This cake has a texture reminiscent of the one I used to love, bringing back sweet memories with every forkful.

Oil spray (optional)

1 large organic orange or 3 small mandarin oranges, unpeeled

1 tablespoon (8 g) organic cornstarch

½ cup (120 ml) water

½ cup (160 g) agave nectar

½ cup (100 g) granulated pure cane sugar

⅔ cup (160 ml) citrus or ginger kombucha or sparkling water

¼ cup (60 ml) extra-virgin olive oil or regular olive oil

½ teaspoon Diamond kosher salt

2 cups (240 g) all-purpose flour

1 tablespoon (12 g) baking powder

1. Preheat the oven to 375°F (190°C, or gas mark 5. Line a 9-inch (23 cm) baking pan with parchment paper, or lightly coat with oil spray.

2. In a small food processor, chop the orange to a pulp. Set aside.

3. In a small microwave-safe bowl, whisk the cornstarch and water to dissolve. Microwave on high power for 1 minute. The mixture will become gelatinous and will give the cake its texture. Let cool for a few minutes.

4. In a large bowl, whisk to combine the orange pulp, cornstarch mixture, agave, sugar, kombucha, oil, and salt.

5. Sift the flour and baking powder on top of the wet ingredients and stir to combine thoroughly. Transfer the batter to the prepared baking pan.

6. Bake until golden brown and set and a toothpick inserted into the center of the cake comes out clean, about 35 minutes.

7. Let cool for at least 15 minutes before transferring the cake from the pan onto a wire rack. Refrigerate before enjoying a slice. I love to serve mine with a layer of citrus jam on top, or a little of The Whole Lemon Curd (page 41). A scoop of vanilla ice cream would be lovely, too.

Yield: 8 servings

PLANET SAVER TIP 92

Make French toast with cake that's going stale. First, ensure it is as stale as can be by cutting thick slices, placing them on a plate, and storing them as is in the refrigerator overnight. Using a blender, combine 1 cup (240 ml) sparkling water (choose an appropriate flavor) with 1 tablespoon (16 g) nut butter of choice, 1 tablespoon (8 g) cornstarch, 2 teaspoons sweetener of choice, ¼ teaspoon baking powder, few grates nutmeg, and a pinch salt. Quickly dip the stale slices of cake in the batter and place in a large heated skillet with butter or oil. Cook over medium heat until golden brown, about 4 minutes per side. If cooking in batches, place the slices in a warm oven while cooking the other batches.

COCONUT PUDDING

Creamy, coconutty perfection. Because sometimes you just need a little something decadent as the closure for the perfect meal. I created this dessert when I had to finish several cans of coconut milk opened for other purposes. Proof number 5929 that there's always a way to find uses for pretty much anything if you put your mind—and your whisk—to it.

⅓ cup (80 ml) favorite creamy plant-based milk

3 tablespoons (24 g) organic cornstarch

1 tablespoon (20 g) white miso

1 (13.5-ounce, or 400 ml) can full-fat coconut milk or cream

½ cup (72 g) coconut sugar or (96 g) Sucanat

Toasted unsweetened thick coconut flakes or shredded coconut

Culinary-grade organic rose buds, for garnish

Dry-roasted pistachios, for garnish

1. In a saucepan, whisk to combine the milk, cornstarch, and miso. Add the coconut milk and coconut sugar. Bring to a boil over medium-high heat. Lower the heat to medium and cook until quite thickened, about 8 minutes, whisking constantly and adjusting the heat as needed to prevent scorching.

2. Transfer the pudding to four small ramekins or bowls and let cool. Apply plastic wrap directly onto the surface of the puddings to prevent them from forming a "skin" on top, and refrigerate until completely set, about 4 hours or overnight. Some folks see the skin as the best part, though—is it worth wasting plastic for that? Up to you.

3. Once ready to serve and properly chilled, garnish with coconut flakes, rose buds, and pistachios.

Yield: 4 small servings

PLANET SAVER TIP 93

As a person living in an area where ants and weevils (a.k.a. my archnemeses) are merciless if what they love to eat isn't stored properly, I strongly urge you to transfer the contents of opened bags of sugar into airtight Mason jars. Not only will it look neater, especially if you create long-lasting labels to make sure you know what's what, it will also keep moisture and anything buggy from getting in there before you do. Once stored properly, you will be able to keep your sugars for at least 1 year.

"COMPOST" COOKIES

No, these aren't made from actual compost matter. Being that we're only two folks in this household and that I clearly love baking, eventually the goods become stale and a little less pleasurable to eat. That's why I prefer smaller yields, but occasionally that just can't happen. So, I throw slightly stale cookies, brownies, chips, and the like in the batter of other cookies to bring them back to life and eat away! Go nuts with what you put in these. Chances are you won't go wrong. I was inspired to use add-ins like those found in a popular, non-vegan cookie made by Christina Tosi of Milk Bar.

1 tablespoon (11 g) whole golden flaxseed, ground

3 tablespoons (45 ml) water

¼ cup (56 g) vegan butter

⅓ cup (67 g) granulated pure cane sugar

⅓ cup (50 g) light brown sugar (not packed), or (64 g) Sucanat

1 cup (120 g) light spelt, all-purpose, or whole-wheat pastry flour

½ teaspoon baking powder

½ teaspoon fine sea salt

Favorite plant-based milk, as needed

6 regular-size vegan marshmallows, cut into s mall bits

¼ cup (50 g) vegan semisweet chocolate chunks

Large handful corn chips (such as Fritos; about 1 ounce, or 28 g)

1. Preheat the oven to 350°F (180°C, or gas mark 4). Line a baking sheet with a silicone baking mat. Alternatively, bake the cookies the next day, after an overnight stay in the fridge for the covered dough. In which case you'll only need to preheat the oven when you're going to bake them, of course.

2. In a small bowl, whisk to combine the flaxseed and water. Let stand a couple of minutes. This will be your flax egg.

3. In a large bowl, using a handheld mixer, cream together the butter and sugars for about 2 minutes. Add the flax egg to the creamed butter and mix to combine.

4. In a separate bowl, sift together the flour, baking powder, and salt. Add the flour mixture to the butter mixture and combine well. The mixture might be dry: add milk, 1 tablespoon (15 ml) at a time, as needed, until the dough sticks together well when pinched. It shouldn't be crumbly or dry, nor should it be too wet. Be sure to add the milk slowly so as not to overmoisten the dough.

5. Using a rubber spatula, gently incorporate the marshmallows, chocolate, and corn chips into the dough. Form the dough into balls, using 2 packed tablespoons (55 g) of dough per cookie. Place the balls on the prepared baking sheet with a good 1 inch (2.5 cm) of space between each, as they do spread a little while baking.

6. Bake for 14 minutes, or until light golden brown. Let cool on the baking sheet for a few minutes before transferring them to a cooling rack. Store the cookies in an airtight container at room temperature, or in the refrigerator, for up to 4 days, or freeze for up to 1 month.

Yield: 10 cookies

PLANET SAVER TIP 94

Cookie dough can be refrigerated or frozen, if you don't want to bake all the cookies the day the dough is prepared. Ideally, form the cookies before freezing so all you have to do is place them on a lined baking sheet and pop them into a hot oven. You will have to bake them a few minutes longer if baking from frozen, so keep an eye on the cookies to adjust the time. Tightly wrap the dough to prevent freezer burn. The frozen dough can be kept up to 3 months in the freezer, and chilled dough can stay up to 1 week in the refrigerator. I should also mention how much I love my countertop toaster oven when the idea of using the big oven isn't tempting. I also use it to roast and broil vegetables with perfect results. Note that it hasn't been proven that it's cheaper or more environmentally friendly, energy-wise, to use a smaller oven.

MOROCCAN CRANACHAN

Cranachan is a Scottish dessert usually composed of whipped cream, toasted oats, whisky, and raspberries. I give it a fresh spin here by combining yogurt with the cream and going for Moroccan flavors using pomegranate, sumac, and rose buds. Not only is it delicious, but it looks gorgeous as well. If you aren't a fan of tart flavors, use something other than pomegranate molasses to sweeten your treat. Agave nectar, brown rice syrup, or even granulated natural sugars will work well here.

⅓ cup (27 g) old-fashioned extra-thick rolled oats

1 cup (240 g) plain or vanilla vegan Greek-style yogurt (sweetened is fine)

Generous 1 cup (50 g) sweetened whipped coconut cream or other vegan whipped cream

6 ounces (170 g) frozen-from-fresh raspberries

¼ cup (40 g) pomegranate arils

Pomegranate molasses, to taste

Pinch ground sumac

¼ cup (30 g) shelled dry-roasted unsalted pistachios

4 ounces (115 g) chopped or crumbled vegan vanilla halva

Dried organic culinary-grade hibiscus flowers, for garnish

Dried organic culinary-grade rose buds or petals, for garnish

Ground turmeric or store-bought mix of golden milk powder, for garnish

1. In a small skillet over medium heat, toast the oats until light golden and fragrant, about 5 minutes. Stir constantly and adjust the heat to prevent burning. Transfer to a small bowl to cool.

2. In a medium-size bowl, fold together the yogurt, whipped cream, cooled oats, two-thirds of the berries (feel free to crumble them slightly for smaller pieces), and two-thirds of the pomegranate arils. Divide among bowls.

3. Top each bowl with a tiny pinch of sumac and divide the remaining raspberries and pomegranate arils among the bowls.

4. Garnish with pistachios, halva, a pinch of hibiscus flowers, a crumble of rose buds or petals, and a tiny pinch of turmeric. Serve immediately.

Yield: 2 to 3 servings

PLANET SAVER TIP 95

During raspberry season, I love to buy more than what's needed because there's no comparing fresh raspberries to store-bought frozen ones: even when you freeze your own raspberries, they are a million times better than those from the store that will inevitably release lots of staining juice once thawed. Those you freeze yourself remain far firmer indeed. For best results, freeze them in a single layer to prevent them from sticking together at a later point. Once frozen, store in an airtight reusable bag and use within 3 months.

SHEET PAN APPLE CRISP

A go-to dessert when apples are a bit too battered for eating by hand. Using a sheet pan instead of a baking dish means more of the crisp part gets a chance to become, well, crisp.

Vegan butter

4 baking apples of choice (see tip, following), chopped into bite-size pieces

⅓ cup (48 g) plus 1½ tablespoons (14 g) coconut sugar or (82 g) Sucanat, divided

2 teaspoons ground cinnamon

1¼ cups (150 g) all-purpose, light spelt, or whole-wheat pastry flour

½ cup (60 g) roasted walnuts or almonds

½ teaspoon Diamond kosher salt

¼ cup (56 g) coconut oil or vegan butter, at room temperature

⅔ cup (160 ml) Salty Beer Caramel Sauce (page 50), as needed

1. Preheat the oven to 375°F (190°C, or gas mark 5). Coat a small rimmed sheet pan (about 8 × 10 inches, or 20 × 25 cm) with butter.

2. Arrange the apples evenly in the prepared pan and evenly top with 1½ tablespoons (14 g) of coconut sugar and the cinnamon.

3. In a food processor, combine the flour, walnuts, remaining ⅓ cup (48 g) of sugar, and salt. Pulse to process until the nuts are finely chopped. Add the coconut oil and pulse just to combine.

4. With the processor running, slowly add the caramel sauce just until the mixture forms a crumble that holds together well when pinched. Distribute the crumble evenly over the apples.

5. Bake for 35 minutes, or until the crumble is golden brown and the apples are fork-tender. Serve warm or at room temperature with whipped coconut cream, a scoop of vanilla ice cream, or as is, as you like.

6. Refrigerate leftovers in an airtight container for up to 3 days. Leftovers can be reheated in a 325°F (170°C, or gas mark 3) oven for 10 minutes or until warmed through.

Yield: 4 to 6 servings

PLANET SAVER TIP 96

I love using smaller apples for cooking and eating. They are usually so much more flavorful than the ridiculously gargantuan-size specimens that can be found at the supermarket. Smaller apples have such a minuscule core that I often end up using the whole thing (pips included, stem out). Feel free to remove anything that doesn't appeal, especially if the apples aren't super small: the results might be uncomfortable to eat. Speaking of appeal, I never peel my apples, even for baking. Do as you prefer.

BEER NUT SHORTBREAD

Always great for dipping in more caramel sauce, enjoy with (caramel?) ice cream, or whatever it is you usually do with shortbread cookies.

1½ cups (180 g) all-purpose flour or whole-wheat pastry flour

Generous ½ cup (100 g) Beer Nut Granola (page 48)

½ teaspoon ground cinnamon (optional)

½ teaspoon Diamond kosher salt

2 tablespoons (28 g) solid coconut oil

2 tablespoons (30 ml) roasted walnut oil or other oil

1 teaspoon pure vanilla extract (optional)

¼ cup (60 ml) Salty Beer Caramel Sauce (page 50)

1. Preheat the oven to 350°F (180°C, or gas mark 4). Line a baking sheet with a silicone baking mat.

2. In a food processor, combine the flour, granola, cinnamon (if using), and salt. Process until the granola is mostly finely ground. Distribute the oils evenly over the flour mixture and add the vanilla (if using). Pulse until just combined. Pea-size bits of flour clumps are welcome.

3. Pour the caramel sauce onto the mixture and pulse just until combined. The mixture should neither be too wet nor too dry. Transfer the mixture onto the silicone mat and shape it into a 4 × 8-inch (10 × 20 cm) rectangle. I like to use a dough scraper to make sure the edges are straight without overheating the dough with my hands. Use the dough scraper to cut the rectangle lengthwise into eight 1-inch (2.5 cm) shortbread fingers. While the fingers are still attached to one another, use a fork to poke holes onto the length of each shortbread cookie. Separate the fingers and reshape with your hands to smooth the sides. Leave the cookies on the silicone mat with 1 inch (2.5 cm) of space between each cookie.

4. Bake for 18 to 20 minutes until golden brown and fragrant. Let cool completely on a wire rack before enjoying. Leftovers can be stored in an airtight container at room temperature, or in the refrigerator, for up to 4 days.

Yield: 8 cookies

PLANET SAVER TIP 97

If you have extra caramel sauce and granola, you can make more of this shortbread prep and use it as a tart shell. I recommend blind baking it before adding the filling to avoid soggy bottoms. Apply the rolled-out dough to a 9-inch (23 cm) tart pan, prick it with a fork, cover it with parchment paper, apply baking weights, and bake in a preheated 350°F (180°C, or gas mark 4) oven for 10 minutes. If you're making a no-bake tart, bake this one fully until golden brown and fragrant, about 16 minutes. Keep an eye on the edges, and if you notice it isn't golden brown enough when removing the weights and parchment paper, put it back in the oven until it is appropriately browned. Don't wander too far to prevent burning.

CHOCOLATE BANANA PEANUT PIE

If the thought of using the banana peels in this decadent pie doesn't appeal (ha), compost them instead. It won't affect the outcome and no one's there to judge you. And if peanut butter's not your favorite, use almond or cashew butter in its place.

FOR CRUST
Oil spray

2 cups (240 g) Chunky Nut Granola (page 31) or other granola of choice

3 tablespoons (36 g) Sucanat or other sweetener of choice

¼ cup (56 g) vegan butter or coconut oil, melted

FOR PIE
3 medium-size ripe organic bananas, skin on, scrubbed clean, patted dry, ends trimmed

1½ cups plus 1 tablespoon (400 g) natural smooth peanut butter

1¼ cups (240 g) Sucanat or other sweetener of choice

⅓ cup (27 g) unsweetened cocoa powder

¼ cup (30 g) all-purpose flour or other flour

½ teaspoon baking powder

Pinch Diamond kosher salt

Plant-based milk, as needed

FOR TOPPING
1¼ cups (220 g) vegan semisweet chocolate chips or chopped bar

½ cup (130 g) natural peanut butter (crunchy or smooth)

¼ cup (80 g) agave nectar

1 tablespoon (15 ml) roasted peanut oil or other oil

Pinch Diamond kosher salt

2 cups (240 g) Chunky Nut Granola (page 31) or other granola of choice

1. To make the crust: Preheat the oven to 350°F (180°C, or gas mark 4). Lightly coat a 9-inch (23 cm) pie plate with oil.

2. In a food processor, combine 1 cup (120 g) of granola and the Sucanat. Process until the granola is coarse. Add the melted butter and pulse to combine. Add the remaining 1 cup (120 g) of granola and pulse to combine until the granola is only coarsely ground. Transfer to the prepared pie plate, pressing down at the bottom and edges. Set aside.

3. To make the pie, using the same food processor, process the bananas until mostly smooth. Add the remaining ingredients and process until smooth. Add a splash of milk at a time if the machine struggles a bit to process the mixture. Stop a few times to scrape down the sides of the bowl with a spatula. Transfer the filling into the crust and spread it evenly.

4. Bake for 30 minutes, or until set. Remove from the oven and let cool on a wire rack.

5. Once the pie is cooled, prepare the topping. In a double boiler, melt the chocolate, peanut butter, agave, oil, and salt. Stir until melted and combined. Add the granola and stir until coated. Place evenly on top of the cooled pie and chill again for at least 4 hours before serving for a crunchy topping, or prepare just before serving for a soft topping.

Yield: 8 servings

PLANET SAVER TIP 98

Yet another recipe willing to work with what's available in your pantry. If you have an old pack of cream-filled cookies, or speculoos-type cookies, use them in the crust instead of the granola. Pretzels are good, too. Note that sugar's optional with the cookies, not so with the pretzels. Use 1½ cups (weight varies) of cookies or pretzels instead of 2 cups (240 g) granola.

PEANUT–FUDGE BROWNIES

Fudgy and deliciously chocolatey, I love these chilled but my husband prefers them at room temperature. If you haven't made the Peanut-Chocolate Fudge (page 168), replace it with the same amount of vegan semisweet chocolate, in chips, chunks, or chopped from a bar.

Oil spray or vegan butter

5 ounces (150 g) shelled roasted chestnuts

2 Medjool dates, pitted

½ cup (120 ml) water or brewed coffee

1 tablespoon (14 g) coconut manna

8½ ounces (240 g) chopped Peanut-Chocolate Fudge (page 168), divided

¼ cup (60 ml) roasted peanut oil or (56 g) coconut oil

1 cup (192 g) Sucanat or (150 g) light brown sugar (not packed)

½ teaspoon fine sea salt

2 teaspoons pure vanilla extract

1 scant cup (105 g) all-purpose flour

¼ cup (22 g) unsweetened cocoa powder

1. Preheat the oven to 350°F (180°C, or gas mark 4). Lightly coat an 8-inch (20 cm) square baking pan with oil or butter. (If you like brownie corners the most, lightly coat two 4 × 8-inch, or 10 × 20 cm, loaf pans with oil. You will need to divide the batter and fudge topping between the two if choosing that option.)

2. In a small saucepan over medium-high heat, combine the chestnuts, dates, water, and coconut manna. Bring to a boil, turn off the heat, and add 4½ ounces (130 g) of fudge. Stir to melt. Let soak for 20 minutes. Transfer to a small food processor, or use an immersion blender, and process until smooth. Transfer to a large bowl.

3. Stir in the oil, Sucanat, salt, and vanilla. Let cool slightly.

4. Sift the flour and cocoa on top, then stir to combine. Transfer the fudge to the prepared pan. Top evenly with the remaining 4 ounces (115 g) of fudge.

5. Bake for 22 minutes until set on top. Let cool completely before slicing. Chill before enjoying, according to your personal preference.

Yield: 8 servings

PLANET SAVER TIP 99

If you're not a fan of oiling your pans because you're trying to avoid extra calories (which I suppose is ironic considering the recipe in question here), line the pans with parchment paper instead. It's a bit less environmentally friendly but I find that parchment paper can often be used more than once in baking applications. If You Care brand sells certified compostable and unbleached parchment baking sheets that are quite reliable, albeit more expensive, compared to regular parchment paper.

PEANUT–CHOCOLATE FUDGE

GF Oh me, oh my. If my partner had to choose one pairing for a dessert item, peanut and chocolate would be it. And if he had to pick one dessert for the rest of his life, fudge might be his choice. Combine it? You get one very happy human being for life. If you aren't a fan of peanuts, note that this is delightful made with roasted almonds and almond butter, roasted cashews and cashew butter, or even roasted hazelnuts and hazelnut butter.

12 ounces (340 g) vegan semisweet chocolate (chips, chunks, or chopped bar)

1 recipe Sweetened Condensed Milk (see tip, following)

½ cup (130 g) natural peanut butter (smooth or crunchy)

1 tablespoon (15 ml) roasted peanut oil

½ cup (60 g) chopped dry-roasted peanuts (I use the broken pieces from the bottom of peanut jars or bulk bags)

Pretzel salt or fleur de sel, to taste

1. Line a small baking pan (9 × 5 inches, or 23 × 13 cm) with parchment paper.

2. In a double-boiler, combine the chocolate, condensed milk, peanut butter, and oil and stir to combine until melted. Remove from heat and stir in the peanuts. Transfer the fudge to the prepared baking pan and use an offset spatula to even out the top.

3. Lightly sprinkle with salt. Refrigerate until set. Cut into small pieces and chill in an airtight container until ready to serve. Keep refrigerated for up to 1 month.

Yield: About 18 pieces

PLANET SAVER TIP 100

Make your own vegan sweetened condensed milk. In a small saucepan over medium heat, stir together 1 (14-ounce, or 425 ml) can full-fat coconut milk, ½ cup (100 g) granulated pure cane sugar, and ½ teaspoon Diamond kosher salt to combine. Cook until thickened and brown, about 1 hour. Stir occasionally and adjust the heat accordingly. Let cool for at least 15 minutes before transferring into a heat-safe jar. Tightly cover and refrigerate for up to 2 weeks. Use anywhere regular sweetened condensed milk is called for. Yield: 1 cup (240 ml)

ANY FRUIT FRANGIPANE GALETTE

SF Here's another recipe I wrote with my mom in mind and heart. I cannot go through apricot season without remembering the wonderful apricot jams and pies she used to make. But I wanted to make this dessert as flexible to fruit availability as possible, so use anything you have at hand, when in season, and munch away.

FOR FRANGIPANE FILLING

½ cup (60 g) almond meal

3 tablespoons (3 g) organic culinary-grade chamomile flowers, crumbled between your fingers into a powder

2 teaspoons organic cornstarch (optional)

½ teaspoon pure almond extract (optional)

¼ cup plus 2 tablespoons (75 g) granulated pure cane sugar, divided

Cold kombucha, flavored sparkling water, or plain water, as needed

6 apricots or plums, or 4 peaches or nectarines, pitted and sliced, or 1½ pounds (681 g) fresh strawberries, hulled and halved

FOR CRUST

1¼ cups (150 g) all-purpose flour

1 tablespoon (12.5 g) granulated pure cane sugar

½ teaspoon Diamond kosher salt

2 teaspoons apple cider vinegar

¼ cup (60 ml) roasted walnut oil or other oil

¼ cup (60 ml) cold kombucha, flavored sparkling water, or plain water, as needed

1. Preheat the oven to 375°F (190°C, or gas mark 5). Have a rimmed baking sheet handy, along with a silicone baking mat or piece of parchment paper.

2. To make the frangipane filling: In a medium-size bowl, combine the almond meal, chamomile, cornstarch (if using; for thicker results, less likely to ooze out of the crust), almond extract (if using; for more genuine frangipane flavor), and ¼ cup (50 g) of sugar. Stir to mix well.

3. Add kombucha, 1 tablespoon (15 ml) at a time, to obtain a somewhat dry paste. I usually need 2 tablespoons (30 ml) of liquid in all. Set aside.

4. In another medium-size bowl, gently stir together the apricots or other fruit and remaining 2 tablespoons (25 g) of sugar to release the juices. Set aside.

Recipe Continues

5. To make the crust: In a medium-size bowl, whisk to combine the flour, sugar, and salt.

6. Add the vinegar and oil. Stir to distribute the oil throughout the flour, creating little pebbles in the process. Do not overwork the dough. Slowly add the kombucha and stir just until a dough forms: it shouldn't be too wet, nor too dry. Transfer to the silicone baking mat or parchment, form the dough into a disk, and roll it into a roughly 10-inch (25 cm) circle. Prick the dough all over with a fork.

7. Place the frangipane mixture evenly in the center, leaving 1½ inches (3.5 cm) from the edge.

8. Drain the extra liquid from the fruit (reserve for smoothies, if desired) and arrange the fruit evenly on top of the frangipane. Use the baking mat or parchment paper to fold the edges of the galette partially over the fruit. Transfer the galette to the baking sheet, using the mat or paper to lift it.

9. Bake for 55 minutes, or until golden brown. Bear in mind the juices might escape, which is a common issue with galettes. Don't sweat it! Rustic is the name of the game. Let cool for 30 minutes before slicing and serving with a big scoop of vanilla ice cream, if desired.

Yield: 4 servings

PLANET SAVER TIP 101

Not fond of chamomile? That's okay, we all have our quirks. Replace it with other teas that might be lurking in the dark recesses of your cupboards. Usually one to two herbal teabags' worth of whatever you have won't be too overwhelming, unless we're going into black tea territory. Show some restraint if using those, about 2 teaspoons to 1 tablespoon (1 g) instead. You don't want the frangipane to take a turn for the bitter.

FUDGY SESAME CHOCOLATE MUG CAKE

If you're in the mood for something decadent but don't want to turn on the huge oven for something small, here's a healthy-ish cake to make in the microwave. You've most certainly heard of those via the internet, and my version is chock-full of sesame: seeds, tahini, and halva. There's nothing more to say except dig in.

3 tablespoons (36 g) Sucanat or (27 g) coconut sugar

2 generous tablespoons (12 g) unsweetened cocoa powder

1 tablespoon (8 g) roasted sesame seeds

2 tablespoons (10 g) quick cooking oats

3 tablespoons (45 ml) plant-based milk of choice or brewed coffee or tea

2 tablespoons (30 g) liquid-y tahini

1½ teaspoons white miso or pinch Diamond kosher salt

⅛ teaspoon baking powder

1½ tablespoons (24 g) vegan halva, crumbled

1 tablespoon (11 g) vegan semisweet chocolate chips

1. Use a coffee grinder or small food processor to process the coconut sugar, cocoa powder, sesame seeds, and oats until finely ground.

2. In a medium-size bowl, whisk to combine the milk, tahini, and miso. Add the ground dry ingredients, baking powder, halva, and chocolate chips to the wet ingredients. Fold to combine. Transfer to a 12-ounce (360 ml) microwave-safe mug and microwave on high power for 60 seconds. The cake should look set and not wet on top: it will remain fudgy inside. Let stand for a couple of minutes before serving, as it will be very hot. Enjoy with any of the following, if desired: a scoop of ice cream, coconut whipped cream, extra chocolate chips, or halva on top.

Yield: 1 mug cake

PLANET SAVER TIP 102

You can alter this recipe to fit what's in your pantry and fridge. Light brown sugar can be used instead of Sucanat, just don't pack it in the tablespoon. Old-fashioned oats can be used instead of quick cooking. Not a fan of tahini? Use roasted cashew or peanut butter instead, just make sure whatever you choose is liquid-y rather than thick. Add-ins can also be replaced by your favorites.

ACKNOWLEDGMENTS

Many thanks to everyone involved in creating this book, especially in these eerie COVID-19 times:

Harvard Common Press and Quarto, Dan Rosenberg, Anne Re, Heather Godin, Jessi Schatz, and Mary Cassells.

Lots of appreciation to past, present, and future testers. That means you, too, Chaz.

Much love and affection to my husband, Chaz, and to our super clingy cat, Willow Rosencat. Welcome home, Harriet, Jiji, and Kiki. Miss you a lot, Buffy Summeowrs. I hope you and Mamou get to hang out together.

To my papa, Michel Narbel. In all this sadness, we were lucky to get to be by her side. Imagine all the people who had to stay away from loved ones struck by illness during the pandemic crisis.

To my sister, brother-in-law, and their kitty: Sandra and Tung Tran-Quang, miaou to you, Kem.

To all the folks who have offered kindness and support when it was needed the most.

To Josette, at the palliative care center of Lavaux Hospital.

To Corinne and family, who were such strong allies while facing their own battle.

Eternal love and gratitude to Monique Narbel-Gimzia for everything she ever was. For the myriad things she's selflessly done for us, that we too often took for granted.

PURVEYORS

Eco-conscious home goods, anything from recycled toothbrushes to reusable bags, to kitchen sponges, and more:

Baggu.com (for reusable, washable grocery bags)

BamboozleHome.com

GIR.co (for those awesome silicone spatulas I mentioned)

HelenMilan.com

JuneHomeSupply.com

PackageFreeShop.com

StasherBag.com (for reusable silicone bags)

TenandCo.ca.

Ceramicists and other makers I adore and whose goods appear quite often in my images and on my table:

CaroleNeilsonCeramic.com

HandselMondays.com

JulieDamhus.dk

NotaryCeramics.com (hi Sarah!)

@rebecca_luerssen (a fantastic woodworker on Instagram)

ShopCupboardGoods.com

UrubuArtisan (another great woodworker, on Etsy)

WhiskeyandClay.com

WonkyPotsbyMae (on Etsy)

and too many more to mention here

ABOUT THE AUTHOR

Celine Steen is a Swiss-born cookbook author who penned *The Complete Guide to Vegan Food Substitutions*, *Bold-Flavored Vegan*, and many more. She's also taken pictures for many cookbooks by other authors. She went vegan in 2005, started a now-dormant food blog (HaveCakeWillTravel.com), and is in awe of the progress made in the plant-based world since then. You can almost always find her styling food and still-life scenes and snapping shots of the results. She lives in Bakersfield, California, with her husband and super-señora cat. You can follow her on Instagram @mmeedamame or see her work on AndBreakfast.net. She can be reached at hello@celinesteen.com.

INDEX

A

almond butter
 AB & Fermented J Pots de Creme, 43
 Banana Berry Smoothie Bowl, 45
 Go-To Nut Butter Dressing, 120
 Savory Sweet Cluck-Free Strips Sand-
  wiches, 87
 Smoky Carrot Spread, 104
almond extract: Any Fruit Frangipane
  Galette, 169–171
almond meal
 Any Fruit Frangipane Galette, 169–171
 Baked Banana Nut Oatmeal, 53
 Flax Crackers, 57
 Trail Mix Cookies, 46
almonds
 Mandarin-White Chocolate Scones, 28
 Sheet Pan Apple Crisp, 164
 Smoky Carrot Spread, 104
apples
 Fennel Kimchi, 117
 Sheet Pan Apple Crisp, 164
 Sloppy Bulgogi, 89
apricots: Any Fruit Frangipane Galette,
  169–171
aquafaba
 Aquafaba Ranch Dressing, 98
 Kimchi-ckpea Stew, 139

B

bananas
 Baked Banana Nut Oatmeal, 53
 Banana Berry Smoothie Bowl, 45
 Breakfast Greena Colada, 35
 Chocolate Banana Peanut Pie, 166
 The Whole Banana-nola Bread, 52
barbecue sauce
 Barbecue Chickpea Scramble, 58
 My Favorite Bowl of Veggies, 84
 Smoky Sausages, 70
 Smoky Sriracha Tacos, 90
 Sriracha Barbecue Sauce, 65
beer
 Baba Ghanoush Soup, 146
 Baked Sweet Potato Bread, 39
 Beet Crumble, 126
 Creton en Croute, 103
 Flax Crackers, 57
 Noochy Sourdough Crackers, 107
 Orange-Habanero Corn Bread, 112

 Plain Jane Sourdough Waffles, 40
 Roasted Onion Soup, 141
 Roasted Potato Beer Salad, 122
 Salty Beer Caramel Sauce, 50
 Savory Pickle Waffles, 129
 Smoky Carrot Spread, 104
 Smoky Sausages, 70
 Sweet and Sour Carrot Tarte Tatin, 78
beets
 Beet Crumble, 126
 Smoky Carrot Meatless Balls, 133
bell peppers
 Mamou's Favorite Miso Bowls, 68–69
 Muhammara, 94
 Pomegranate Ezme, 132
 Root Veggie Gumbo, 148
 Ropa Vieja Tacos, 99
 Sunset Stew, 147
black beans
 Finishing Brown Sauce, 136
 Mushroom Corn Chip Chili, 150
 Spicy Bean Burgers, 81
blackstrap molasses
 Baked Sweet Potato Bread, 39
 Coconut Carrot Cookies, 29
 Savory Sweet Cluck-Free Strips
  Sandwiches, 87
 Sriracha Barbecue Sauce, 65
blueberries
 AB & Fermented J Pots de Creme, 43
 Banana Berry Smoothie Bowl, 45
bok choy: Mamou's Favorite Miso Bowls,
  68–69
broccoli
 Mamou's Favorite Miso Bowls, 68–69
 My Favorite Bowl of Veggies, 84
 Pineapple Fried Rice, 93
Brussels sprouts: My Favorite Bowl of
  Veggies, 84
buckwheat groats: Beer Nut Granola, 48
butternut squash: Butternut Squash
  Lasagna, 96–97

C

cabbage
 Chaat Masala Chickpea Pockets, 63
 Everything but the Kitchen Sink Left-
  over Veggies Stew, 138
 Moroccan Quinoa Veggie Bowl, 73–74
 My Favorite Bowl of Veggies, 84
 Ropa Vieja Tacos, 99

 Sloppy Bulgogi, 89
 Smoky Sriracha Tacos, 90
 Yuzu Koji Tempeh Sandwiches, 67
caramel sauce
 Beer Nut Granola, 48
 Beer Nut Shortbread, 165
 Miso Caramel Spread, 51
 Salty Beer Caramel Sauce, 50
 Sheet Pan Apple Crisp, 164
carrots
 Basil–Carrot Top Pesto, 109
 Coconut Carrot Cookies, 29
 Everything but the Kitchen Sink
  Leftover Veggies Stew, 138
 A Guide to Veggie Broth, 142–143
 Mamou's Favorite Miso Bowls, 68–69
 Muhammara, 94
 My Favorite Bowl of Veggies, 84
 Pickled Turmeric Carrots, 114
 Queso'rprise, 118
 Smoky Carrot Meatless Balls, 133
 Smoky Carrot Spread, 104
 Sweet and Sour Carrot Tarte Tatin, 78
 Yuzu Koji Tempeh Sandwiches, 67
 Za'atar Chutney, 125
cashew butter
 Go-To Nut Butter Dressing, 120
 Pineapple Berry Swirl Smoothie, 38
 Savory Sweet Cluck-Free Strips
  Sandwiches, 87
cashews
 Beer Nut Granola, 48
 Breakfast Rice Pudding, 32
 Cashew Sour Cream and Lasagna
  Sauce, 95
 Kimchi Fried "Noodz," 88
 Queso'rprise, 118
cauliflower
 My Favorite Bowl of Veggies, 84
 Pistachio Dukkah Whole
  Cauliflower, 83
 Queso'rprise, 118
celeriac
 Baba Ghanoush Soup, 146
 Roasted Potato Beer Salad, 122
 Zippy Herb Dressing, 75
celery
 A Guide to Veggie Broth, 142–143
 Root Veggie Gumbo, 148–149
chaat masala
 Chaat Masala Chickpea Pockets, 63

Chaat Masala Peas and Quinoa
    Stew, 62
chestnuts: Peanut-Fudge Brownies, 167
chia seeds
    Flax Crackers, 57
    Lemon Curd Muffins, 42
    Overnight Strawberry Chia Jam, 38
    Pineapple Berry Swirl Smoothie, 38
chickpea flour
    Herby Quinoa Frittata, 66
    Smoky Sausages, 70
chickpeas
    Barbecue Chickpea Scramble, 58
    Chaat Masala Chickpea Pockets, 63
    Cocoa Nut Hummus, 30
    Everything but the Kitchen Sink
        Leftover Veggies Stew, 138
    Kimchi-ckpea Stew, 139
    Moroccan Quinoa Veggie Bowl, 73–74
    My Favorite Bowl of Veggies, 84
    Olive Fennel Hummus, 108
    Sunset Stew, 147
    Uncanny Chickpeas, 145
chocolate
    Baked Banana Nut Oatmeal, 53
    Chocolate Banana Peanut Pie, 166
    "Compost" Cookies, 160–161
    Fudgy Sesame Chocolate Mug Cake,
        172
    Mandarin-White Chocolate Scones, 28
    Peanut-Chocolate Fudge, 168
chutney
    Chaat Masala Chickpea Pockets, 63
    Pineapple Tamarind Chutney, 64
    Za'atar Chutney, 125
cinnamon
    Beer Nut Shortbread, 165
    Coconut Carrot Cookies, 29
    Pulled Jackfruit Sandwiches, 71
    Sheet Pan Apple Crisp, 164
    Soured-Oat Hand Waffles, 34
    Trail Mix Cookies, 46
cocoa powder
    Chocolate Banana Peanut Pie, 166
    Chunky Nut Granola, 31
    Cocoa Nut Hummus, 30
    Fudgy Sesame Chocolate Mug Cake,
        172
    Peanut-Fudge Brownies, 167
coconut cream
    Coconut Pudding, 159
    Moroccan Cranachan, 162
    Salty Beer Caramel Sauce, 50
coconut flakes
    Beer Nut Granola, 48
    Breakfast Rice Pudding, 32
    Coconut Carrot Cookies, 29
    Coconut Pudding, 159
    Pickled Turmeric Carrots, 114
coconut manna
    Breakfast Greena Colada, 35

Miso Caramel Spread, 51
Peanut-Fudge Brownies, 167
Pineapple Berry Swirl Smoothie, 38
Pink Latte, 37
Queso'rprise, 118
The Whole Lemon Curd, 41
coconut milk
    AB & Fermented J Pots de Creme, 43
    Breakfast Rice Pudding, 32
    Carrot Top–Pea Soup with Pesto, 153
    Coconut Pudding, 159
    Everything but the Kitchen Sink Left-
        over Veggies Stew, 138
    Kimchi-ckpea Stew, 139
    Red Curry Peanut Sauce, 113
coconut sugar
    Baked Banana Nut Oatmeal, 53
    Chunky Nut Granola, 31
    Coconut Carrot Cookies, 29
    Coconut Pudding, 159
    Finishing Brown Sauce, 136
    Fudgy Sesame Chocolate Mug
        Cake, 172
    Pineapple Tamarind Chutney, 64
    Red Curry Peanut Sauce, 113
    Sheet Pan Apple Crisp, 164
    Soured-Oat Hand Waffles, 34
    Sriracha Barbecue Sauce, 65
    Trail Mix Cookies, 46
coconut water
    Herby Quinoa Frittata, 66
    Pistachio Dukkah Whole
        Cauliflower, 83
    Queso'rprise, 118
    Trail Mix Cookies, 46
coffee
    Fudgy Sesame Chocolate Mug
        Cake, 172
    Peanut-Fudge Brownies, 167
corn chips
    "Compost" Cookies, 160–161
    Mushroom Corn Chip Chili, 150
    Spicy Bean Burgers, 81
cremini mushrooms: Mushroom Corn
    Chip Chili, 150
cucumbers
    Chaat Masala Chickpea Pockets, 63
    Pomegranate Ezme, 132
    Pulled Jackfruit Sandwiches, 71
    Yuzu Koji Tempeh Sandwiches, 67
curry paste: Red Curry Peanut Sauce, 113

D
dashi
    Mamou's Favorite Miso Bowls, 68–69
    Savory Sweet Cluck-Free Strips
        Sandwiches, 87
dates
    Baked Banana Nut Oatmeal, 53
    Miso Caramel Spread, 51

Peanut-Fudge Brownies, 167
Pink Latte, 37

E
eggplant
    Baba Ghanoush Soup, 146
    Moroccan Quinoa Veggie Bowl, 73–74
    My Favorite Bowl of Veggies, 84

F
fennel
    Fennel Kimchi, 117
    A Guide to Veggie Broth, 142–143
    Olive Fennel Hummus, 108
    Savory Pickle Waffles, 129
    Tomato Hummus Soup, 154
FF (fast-forward) recipes
    Aquafaba Ranch Dressing, 98
    Banana Berry Smoothie Bowl, 45
    Basil–Carrot Top Pesto, 109
    Breakfast Greena Colada, 35
    Carrot Top–Pea Soup with Pesto, 153
    Cocoa Nut Hummus, 30
    Mandarin-White Chocolate Scones, 28
    Miso Caramel Spread, 51
    Pineapple Berry Swirl Smoothie, 38
    Pink Latte, 37
    Umami Sofrito, 119
    Za'atar Chutney, 125
    Zippy Herb Dressing, 75
flaxseed
    Chunky Nut Granola, 31
    "Compost" Cookies, 160–161
    Flax Crackers, 57
    Plain Jane Sourdough Waffles, 40
    Soured-Oat Hand Waffles, 34
    Trail Mix Cookies, 46

G
garlic
    Aquafaba Ranch Dressing, 98
    Barbecue Chickpea Scramble, 58
    Basil–Carrot Top Pesto, 109
    Butternut Squash Lasagna, 96–97
    Carrot Top–Pea Soup with Pesto, 153
    Cashew Sour Cream and Lasagna
        Sauce, 95
    Chaat Masala Chickpea Pockets, 63
    Chaat Masala Peas and Quinoa
        Stew, 62
    Congee Bowl, 55–56
    Creton, 102
    Fennel Kimchi, 117
    Finishing Brown Sauce, 136
    Go-To Nut Butter Dressing, 120
    A Guide to Veggie Broth, 142–143
    Kimchi-ckpea Stew, 139
    Kimchi Fried "Noodz," 88
    Mamou's Favorite Miso Bowls, 68–69

Moroccan Quinoa Veggie Bowl, 73–74
Muhammara, 94
Pineapple Fried Rice, 93
Pomegranate Ezme, 132
Potato Roesti, 128
Pulled Jackfruit Sandwiches, 71
Red Curry Peanut Sauce, 113
Roasted Onion Soup, 141
Roasted Potato Beer Salad, 122
Root Veggie Gumbo, 148–149
Ropa Vieja Tacos, 99
Sichuan-Flavored Mushrooms with
    Roasted Shishito Peppers, 77
Sloppy Bulgogi, 89
Smoky Sriracha Tacos, 90
Spicy Glazed Root Veggies, 124
Sunset Stew, 147
Tomato Hummus Soup, 154
Umami Sofrito, 119
Uncanny Chickpeas, 145
Za'atar Chutney, 125
Zippy Herb Dressing, 75
GF (gluten-free recipes)
AB & Fermented J Pots de Creme, 43
Baked Banana Nut Oatmeal, 53
Banana Berry Smoothie Bowl, 45
Basil–Carrot Top Pesto, 109
Breakfast Greena Colada, 35
Breakfast Rice Pudding, 32
Carrot Top–Pea Soup with Pesto, 153
Cashew Sour Cream and Lasagna
    Sauce, 95
Chaat Masala Peas and Quinoa
    Stew, 62
Cocoa Nut Hummus, 30
Herby Quinoa Frittata, 66
Moroccan Quinoa Veggie Bowl, 73–74
Muhammara, 94
Olive Fennel Hummus, 108
Orange-Habanero Jam, 110
Peanut-Chocolate Fudge, 168
Pickled Red Onions, 115
Pickled Turmeric Carrots, 114
Pineapple Tamarind Chutney, 64
Pink Latte, 37
Pomegranate Ezme, 132
Potato Roesti, 128
Umami Sofrito, 119
The Whole Lemon Curd, 41
Za'atar Chutney, 125
Zippy Herb Dressing, 75
ginger
Breakfast Rice Pudding, 32
Carrot Top–Pea Soup with Pesto, 153
Finishing Brown Sauce, 136
Mamou's Favorite Miso Bowls, 68–69
Pickled Turmeric Carrots, 114
Pineapple Tamarind Chutney, 64
Sichuan-Flavored Mushrooms with
    Roasted Shishito Peppers, 77
Sloppy Bulgogi, 89

Smoky Sriracha Tacos, 90
Soured-Oat Hand Waffles, 34
Gochujang Paste
Go-To Nut Butter Dressing, 120
Sloppy Bulgogi, 89
Spicy Glazed Root Veggies, 124
golden milk powder
Breakfast Rice Pudding, 32
Moroccan Cranachan, 162
Soured-Oat Hand Waffles, 34
granola
Banana Berry Smoothie Bowl, 45
Beer Nut Granola, 48
Beer Nut Shortbread, 165
Chocolate Banana Peanut Pie, 166
Chunky Nut Granola, 31
Overnight Granola Bowl, 44
Trail Mix Cookies, 46
The Whole Banana-nola Bread, 52
greens
Kimchi-ckpea Stew, 139
Kimchi Fried "Noodz," 88
Mamou's Favorite Miso Bowls, 68–69
Moroccan Quinoa Veggie Bowl, 73–74
Pineapple Fried Rice, 93

H

habanero peppers
Orange-Habanero Corn Bread, 112
Orange-Habanero Jam, 110
Root Veggie Gumbo, 148–149
Savory Sweet Cluck-Free Strips
    Sandwiches, 87
Sunset Stew, 147
halva
Breakfast Rice Pudding, 32
Fudgy Sesame Chocolate Mug
    Cake, 172
Halva Scones, 47
Moroccan Cranachan, 162
harissa spice
Baba Ghanoush Soup, 146
Moroccan Quinoa Veggie Bowl, 73–74
Pistachio Dukkah Whole
    Cauliflower, 83
hummus
Cocoa Nut Hummus, 30
Olive Fennel Hummus, 108
Tomato Hummus Soup, 154

J

jackfruit
Congee Bowl, 55–56
Pulled Jackfruit Sandwiches, 71
Ropa Vieja Tacos, 99
jam
Orange-Habanero Corn Bread, 112
Orange-Habanero Jam, 110
Overnight Granola Bowl, 44
Overnight Strawberry Chia Jam, 38

Pineapple Berry Swirl Smoothie, 38
Savory Sweet Cluck-Free Strips
    Sandwiches, 87

K

kale
Barbecue Chickpea Scramble, 58
Breakfast Greena Colada, 35
Kimchi-ckpea Stew, 139
Mamou's Favorite Miso Bowls, 68–69
kidney beans
Mushroom Corn Chip Chili, 150
Ropa Vieja Tacos, 99
kimchi
Congee Bowl, 55–56
Fennel Kimchi, 117
Kimchi-ckpea Stew, 139
Kimchi Fried "Noodz," 88
My Favorite Bowl of Veggies, 84
Sloppy Bulgogi, 89
Smoky Sausages, 70
kombu
Congee Bowl, 55–56
Mamou's Favorite Miso Bowls, 68–69
kombucha
Any Fruit Frangipane Galette, 169–171
Citrus Quark-alike Cake, 158
Plain Jane Sourdough Waffles, 40
Smoky Sausages, 70
Soured-Oat Hand Waffles, 34

L

Labneh
AB & Fermented J Pots de Creme, 43
Beet Crumble, 126
recipe, 127
lemon curd
Lemon Curd Muffins, 42
The Whole Lemon Curd, 41
lemon juice
AB & Fermented J Pots de Creme, 43
Basil–Carrot Top Pesto, 109
Breakfast Rice Pudding, 32
Cashew Sour Cream and Lasagna
    Sauce, 95
Chaat Masala Chickpea Pockets, 63
Miso Sake Sauce, 121
Olive Fennel Hummus, 108
Smoky Carrot Spread, 104
Za'atar Chutney, 125
Zippy Herb Dressing, 75
lemons
A Guide to Veggie Broth, 142–143
Uncanny Chickpeas, 145
lentils
Everything but the Kitchen Sink Left-
    over Veggies Stew, 138
Sloppy Bulgogi, 89
lime juice
AB & Fermented J Pots de Creme, 43
Breakfast Greena Colada, 35

Fennel Kimchi, 117
Queso'rprise, 118
Red Curry Peanut Sauce, 113
Smoky Carrot Spread, 104

M

maca powder
    Basil–Carrot Top Pesto, 109
    Cashew Sour Cream and Lasagna
        Sauce, 95
    Flax Crackers, 57
    Queso'rprise, 118
mandarin oranges
    Citrus Quark-alike Cake, 158
    Mandarin-White Chocolate Scones, 28
mayo
    Aquafaba Ranch Dressing, 98
    Pulled Jackfruit Sandwiches, 71
    Roasted Potato Beer Salad, 122
    Ropa Vieja Tacos, 99
    Sloppy Bulgogi, 89
    Yuzu Koji Tempeh Sandwiches, 67
mirin
    Miso Sake Sauce, 121
    Sriracha Barbecue Sauce, 65
miso
    Baba Ghanoush Soup, 146
    Butternut Squash Lasagna, 96–97
    Cashew Sour Cream and Lasagna
        Sauce, 95
    Chaat Masala Peas and Quinoa Stew,
        62
    Coconut Pudding, 159
    Creton, 102
    Fudgy Sesame Chocolate Mug Cake,
        172
    Go-To Nut Butter Dressing, 120
    introduction to, 22
    Kimchi-ckpea Stew, 139
    Mamou's Favorite Miso Bowls, 68–69
    Miso Caramel Spread, 51
    Miso Sake Sauce, 121
    Sunset Stew, 147
molasses
    Baba Ghanoush Soup, 146
    Baked Sweet Potato Bread, 39
    Beet Crumble, 126
    Breakfast Rice Pudding, 32
    Coconut Carrot Cookies, 29
    Labneh, 127
    Moroccan Quinoa Veggie Bowl, 73–74
    Overnight Strawberry Chia Jam, 38
    Pineapple Berry Swirl Smoothie, 38
    Pomegranate Ezme, 132
    Savory Sweet Cluck-Free Strips Sand-
        wiches, 87
    Sriracha Barbecue Sauce, 65
    Sweet and Sour Carrot Tarte Tatin, 78
mushroom powder
    Chaat Masala Peas and Quinoa
        Stew, 62

Herby Quinoa Frittata, 66
Kimchi-ckpea Stew, 139
Pulled Jackfruit Sandwiches, 71
Queso'rprise, 118
Root Veggie Gumbo, 148–149
Ropa Vieja Tacos, 99
Sichuan-Flavored Mushrooms with
    Roasted Shishito Peppers, 77
Smoky Sausages, 70
Spicy Bean Burgers, 81
Tomato Hummus Soup, 154
mushrooms
    Barbecue Chickpea Scramble, 58
    Butternut Squash Lasagna, 96–97
    Congee Bowl, 55–56
    Mushroom Corn Chip Chili, 150
    Sichuan-Flavored Mushrooms with
        Roasted Shishito Peppers, 77
    Sloppy Bulgogi, 89
    Smoky Sriracha Tacos, 90
    Umami Sofrito, 119
mushroom soaking liquid
    Cashew Sour Cream and Lasagna
        Sauce, 95
    Creton, 102

N

nectarines: Any Fruit Frangipane Galette,
    169–171
noodles
    Kimchi Fried "Noodz," 88
    Mamou's Favorite Miso Bowls, 68–69
nutmeg
    Butternut Squash Lasagna, 96–97
    Cashew Sour Cream and Lasagna
        Sauce, 95
    Coconut Carrot Cookies, 29
nutritional yeast
    Cashew Sour Cream and Lasagna
        Sauce, 95
    Chaat Masala Peas and Quinoa
        Stew, 62
    Creton, 102
    Herby Quinoa Frittata, 66
    introduction to, 22
    Noochy Sourdough Crackers, 107
    Queso'rprise, 118
    Savory Sweet Cluck-Free Strips Sand-
        wiches, 87
    Smoky Carrot Meatless Balls, 133
    Smoky Sausages, 70
    Spicy Bean Burgers, 81

O

oats
    Baked Banana Nut Oatmeal, 53
    Beer Nut Granola, 48
    Chunky Nut Granola, 31
    Coconut Carrot Cookies, 29
    Creton, 102

Fudgy Sesame Chocolate Mug Cake,
    172
Moroccan Cranachan, 162
Pineapple Berry Swirl Smoothie, 38
Soured-Oat Hand Waffles, 34
Spicy Bean Burgers, 81
olive oil
    Baked Sweet Potato Bread, 39
    Basil–Carrot Top Pesto, 109
    Beet Crumble, 126
    Chaat Masala Chickpea Pockets, 63
    Chili Mac Gratin, 82
    Citrus Quark-alike Cake, 158
    Creton en Croute, 103
    A Guide to Veggie Broth, 142–143
    Labneh, 127
    Lemon Curd Muffins, 42
    Muhammara, 94
    Olive Fennel Hummus, 108
    Orange-Habanero Corn Bread, 112
    Plain Jane Sourdough Waffles, 40
    Pomegranate Ezme, 132
    Roasted Onion Soup, 141
    Root Veggie Gumbo, 148–149
    Ropa Vieja Tacos, 99
    Spicy Bean Burgers, 81
    Sweet and Sour Carrot Tarte Tatin, 78
    Umami Sofrito, 119
    Uncanny Chickpeas, 145
    The Whole Banana-nola Bread, 52
    Za'atar Chutney, 125
    Zippy Herb Dressing, 75
olives
    Labneh, 127
    Olive Fennel Hummus, 108
    Pomegranate Ezme, 132
onion powder
    Aquafaba Ranch Dressing, 98
    Cashew Sour Cream and Lasagna
        Sauce, 95
    Pineapple Tamarind Chutney, 64
    Queso'rprise, 118
    Savory Pickle Waffles, 129
    Savory Sweet Cluck-Free Strips Sand-
        wiches, 87
    Smoky Carrot Meatless Balls, 133
    Smoky Carrot Spread, 104
    Smoky Sausages, 70
    Spicy Bean Burgers, 81
    Sriracha Barbecue Sauce, 65
onion purée
    Baba Ghanoush Soup, 146
    Carrot Top–Pea Soup with Pesto, 153
onions
    Chaat Masala Peas and Quinoa
        Stew, 62
    Creton, 102
    Finishing Brown Sauce, 136
    A Guide to Veggie Broth, 142–143
    Moroccan Quinoa Veggie Bowl, 73–74
    Muhammara, 94

My Favorite Bowl of Veggies, 84
Pickled Red Onions, 115
Pomegranate Ezme, 132
Roasted Onion Soup, 141
Roasted Potato Beer Salad, 122
Root Veggie Gumbo, 148–149
Ropa Vieja Tacos, 99
Sunset Stew, 147
orange juice: Breakfast Greena
    Colada, 35
oranges
Citrus Quark-alike Cake, 158
Mandarin-White Chocolate Scones, 28
Orange-Habanero Corn Bread, 112
Orange-Habanero Jam, 110
Pomegranate Ezme, 132

P

pasta
Butternut Squash Lasagna, 96–97
Chili Mac Gratin, 82
Kimchi Fried "Noodz," 88
peaches: Any Fruit Frangipane Galette,
    169–171
peanut butter
Baked Banana Nut Oatmeal, 53
Chocolate Banana Peanut Pie, 166
Chunky Nut Granola, 31
Go-To Nut Butter Dressing, 120
Peanut-Chocolate Fudge, 168
Savory Sweet Cluck-Free Strips
    Sandwiches, 87
Sunset Stew, 147
peanut oil
Baked Banana Nut Oatmeal, 53
Beer Nut Granola, 48
Beet Crumble, 126
Butternut Squash Lasagna, 96–97
Chaat Masala Chickpea Pockets, 63
Chili Mac Gratin, 82
Chocolate Banana Peanut Pie, 166
Chunky Nut Granola, 31
Coconut Carrot Cookies, 29
Herby Quinoa Frittata, 66
Kimchi Fried "Noodz," 88
Miso Caramel Spread, 51
Orange-Habanero Corn Bread, 112
Peanut-Chocolate Fudge, 168
Peanut-Fudge Brownies, 167
Pineapple Fried Rice, 93
Pistachio Dukkah Whole
    Cauliflower, 83
Ropa Vieja Tacos, 99
Smoky Sriracha Tacos, 90
Soured-Oat Hand Waffles, 34
Umami Sofrito, 119
Yuzu Koji Tempeh Sandwiches, 67
peanuts
Beer Nut Granola, 48
Kimchi Fried "Noodz," 88

Peanut-Chocolate Fudge, 168
Red Curry Peanut Sauce, 113
Sichuan-Flavored Mushrooms with
    Roasted Shishito Peppers, 77
pearl onions
A Guide to Veggie Broth, 142–143
Moroccan Quinoa Veggie Bowl, 73–74
pears: Sloppy Bulgogi, 89
peas
Carrot Top–Pea Soup with Pesto, 153
Chaat Masala Peas and Quinoa
    Stew, 62
Creton, 102
pecans: Beer Nut Granola, 48
pesto
Basil–Carrot Top Pesto, 109
Herby Quinoa Frittata, 66
pineapple
Breakfast Greena Colada, 35
Breakfast Rice Pudding, 32
Finishing Brown Sauce, 136
Pineapple Berry Swirl Smoothie, 38
Pineapple Fried Rice, 93
Pineapple Tamarind Chutney, 64
pineapple juice
Finishing Brown Sauce, 136
Orange-Habanero Jam, 110
pine nuts
Basil–Carrot Top Pesto, 109
Chaat Masala Chickpea Pockets, 63
Moroccan Quinoa Veggie Bowl, 73–74
pistachios
Beet Crumble, 126
Chaat Masala Chickpea Pockets, 63
Coconut Pudding, 159
Halva Scones, 47
Moroccan Cranachan, 162
Moroccan Quinoa Veggie Bowl, 73–74
Pistachio Dukkah Whole
    Cauliflower, 83
Sweet and Sour Carrot Tarte Tatin, 78
plantain chips: Ropa Vieja Tacos, 99
plant-based milk
Baked Banana Nut Oatmeal, 53
Banana Berry Smoothie Bowl, 45
Breakfast Greena Colada, 35
Breakfast Rice Pudding, 32
Coconut Pudding, 159
"Compost" Cookies, 160–161
Fudgy Sesame Chocolate Mug
    Cake, 172
Halva Scones, 47
Mandarin-White Chocolate Scones, 28
Overnight Granola Bowl, 44
Pineapple Berry Swirl Smoothie, 38
Soured-Oat Hand Waffles, 34
Trail Mix Cookies, 46
The Whole Banana-nola Bread, 52
plums: Any Fruit Frangipane Galette,
    169–171
pomegranate arils

Baba Ghanoush Soup, 146
Labneh, 127
Moroccan Cranachan, 162
Pomegranate Ezme, 132
pomegranate molasses
Baba Ghanoush Soup, 146
Beet Crumble, 126
Breakfast Rice Pudding, 32
Labneh, 127
Moroccan Cranachan, 162
Moroccan Quinoa Veggie Bowl, 73–74
Overnight Strawberry Chia Jam, 38
Pineapple Berry Swirl Smoothie, 38
Pomegranate Ezme, 132
Sweet and Sour Carrot Tarte Tatin, 78
pomegranate seeds
Breakfast Rice Pudding, 32
Moroccan Quinoa Veggie Bowl, 73–74
Overnight Strawberry Chia Jam, 38
Pineapple Berry Swirl Smoothie, 38
porcini mushroom powder
Spicy Bean Burgers, 81
Tomato Hummus Soup, 154
portobello mushrooms: Kimchi-ckpea
    Stew, 139
portobello mushroom powder
Chaat Masala Peas and Quinoa
    Stew, 62
Creton, 102
Ropa Vieja Tacos, 99
potatoes
Everything but the Kitchen Sink Left-
    over Veggies Stew, 138
Potato Roesti, 128
Queso'rprise, 118
Roasted Potato Beer Salad, 122

Q

queso
Chili Mac Gratin, 82
Mushroom Corn Chip Chili, 150
Queso'rprise, 118
quince jelly: Go-To Nut Butter
    Dressing, 120
quinoa
Chaat Masala Chickpea Pockets, 63
Chaat Masala Peas and Quinoa
    Stew, 62
Herby Quinoa Frittata, 66
Moroccan Quinoa Veggie Bowl, 73–74

R

radicchio: My Favorite Bowl of
    Veggies, 84
radishes: Yuzu Koji Tempeh
    Sandwiches, 67
raisins
Baked Banana Nut Oatmeal, 53
Coconut Carrot Cookies, 29
Pineapple Tamarind Chutney, 64

Soured-Oat Hand Waffles, 34
Trail Mix Cookies, 46
raspberries: Moroccan Cranachan, 162
red onions
Moroccan Quinoa Veggie Bowl, 73–74
Muhammara, 94
My Favorite Bowl of Veggies, 84
Pickled Red Onions, 115
Pomegranate Ezme, 132
Roasted Onion Soup, 141
Roasted Potato Beer Salad, 122
Ropa Vieja Tacos, 99
rice
Breakfast Rice Pudding, 32
Chaat Masala Peas and Quinoa
Stew, 62
Congee Bowl, 55–56
Pineapple Fried Rice, 93
rum: Pineapple Tamarind Chutney, 64
rutabaga
Everything but the Kitchen Sink Left-
over Veggies Stew, 138
Root Veggie Gumbo, 148–149

S

sake sauce
Miso Sake Sauce, 121
Smoky Carrot Meatless Balls, 133
Smoky Sausages, 70
sausage
Pineapple Fried Rice, 93
Root Veggie Gumbo, 148–149
Smoky Sausages, 70
Smoky Sriracha Tacos, 90
scallions
Chili Mac Gratin, 82
Congee Bowl, 55–56
Fennel Kimchi, 117
Kimchi Fried "Noodz," 88
Mamou's Favorite Miso Bowls, 68–69
Pineapple Fried Rice, 93
Sichuan-Flavored Mushrooms with
Roasted Shishito Peppers, 77
Sloppy Bulgogi, 89
Sour Cream Onion Scones, 131
serrano peppers
Pineapple Tamarind Chutney, 64
Ropa Vieja Tacos, 99
sesame seeds
Congee Bowl, 55–56
Flax Crackers, 57
Fudgy Sesame Chocolate
Mug Cake, 172
Halva Scones, 47
Sloppy Bulgogi, 89
Smoky Sriracha Tacos, 90
Za'atar Chutney, 125
SF (soy-free) recipes
Any Fruit Frangipane Galette, 169–171
Baked Sweet Potato Bread, 39

Basil–Carrot Top Pesto, 109
Beer Nut Granola, 48
Breakfast Greena Colada, 35
Breakfast Rice Pudding, 32
Carrot Top–Pea Soup with Pesto, 153
Cashew Sour Cream and Lasagna
Sauce, 95
Citrus Quark-alike Cake, 158
Cocoa Nut Hummus, 30
Flax Crackers, 57
Muhammara, 94
Olive Fennel Hummus, 108
Orange-Habanero Corn Bread, 112
Orange-Habanero Jam, 110
Pickled Red Onions, 115
Pickled Turmeric Carrots, 114
Pineapple Tamarind Chutney, 64
Pink Latte, 37
Pistachio Dukkah Whole
Cauliflower, 83
Plain Jane Sourdough Waffles, 40
Pomegranate Ezme, 132
Potato Roesti, 128
Salty Beer Caramel Sauce, 50
Savory Pickle Waffles, 129
Smoky Carrot Spread, 104
Umami Sofrito, 119
The Whole Lemon Curd, 41
Za'atar Chutney, 125
Zippy Herb Dressing, 75
shallots
Barbecue Chickpea Scramble, 58
Butternut Squash Lasagna, 96–97
Kimchi-ckpea Stew, 139
Muhammara, 94
Mushroom Corn Chip Chili, 150
Pineapple Fried Rice, 93
Pineapple Tamarind Chutney, 64
Potato Roesti, 128
Smoky Sriracha Tacos, 90
Spicy Glazed Root Veggies, 124
Tomato Hummus Soup, 154
Umami Sofrito, 119
shelf life, 24–25
shiitake mushroom powder
Chaat Masala Peas and Quinoa
Stew, 62
Creton, 102
Spicy Bean Burgers, 81
shiitake mushrooms
Barbecue Chickpea Scramble, 58
Butternut Squash Lasagna, 96–97
Congee Bowl, 55–56
Kimchi-ckpea Stew, 139
Sichuan-Flavored Mushrooms with
Roasted Shishito Peppers, 77
Sloppy Bulgogi, 89
Smoky Sriracha Tacos, 90
shio koji: Yuzu Koji Tempeh
Sandwiches, 67
shishito peppers: Sichuan-Flavored

Mushrooms with Roasted
Shishito Peppers, 77
smoothies
Banana Berry Smoothie Bowl, 45
Breakfast Greena Colada, 35
Pineapple Berry Swirl Smoothie, 38
Pink Latte, 37
sofrito
Mushroom Corn Chip Chili, 150
Sloppy Bulgogi, 89
Spicy Glazed Root Veggies, 124
Tomato Hummus Soup, 154
Umami Sofrito, 119
sour cream
Aquafaba Ranch Dressing, 98
Butternut Squash Lasagna, 96–97
Cashew Sour Cream, 95
Chaat Masala Chickpea Pockets, 63
Herby Quinoa Frittata, 66
Roasted Onion Soup, 141
Sour Cream Onion Scones, 131
Spicy Bean Burgers, 81
sourdough
Halva Scones, 47
Noochy Sourdough Crackers, 107
Plain Jane Sourdough Waffles, 40
Soured-Oat Hand Waffles, 34
soy curls: Savory Sweet Cluck-Free Strips
Sandwiches, 87
soy sauce
Congee Bowl, 55–56
Red Curry Peanut Sauce, 113
Savory Sweet Cluck-Free Strips
Sandwiches, 87
spinach
Breakfast Greena Colada, 35
Chaat Masala Chickpea Pockets, 63
Mamou's Favorite Miso Bowls, 68–69
squash
Butternut Squash Lasagna, 96–97
Everything but the Kitchen Sink Left-
over Veggies Stew, 138
Moroccan Quinoa Veggie Bowl, 73–74
My Favorite Bowl of Veggies, 84
sriracha
Mamou's Favorite Miso Bowls, 68–69
Pineapple Fried Rice, 93
Savory Sweet Cluck-Free Strips
Sandwiches, 87
Sriracha Barbecue Sauce, 65
strawberries
Any Fruit Frangipane Galette, 169–171
Breakfast Rice Pudding, 32
Overnight Strawberry Chia Jam, 38
Pineapple Berry Swirl Smoothie, 38
Pink Latte, 37
sunflower seeds
Baked Sweet Potato Bread, 39
Beet Crumble, 126
Trail Mix Cookies, 46
sweet potatoes

Baked Sweet Potato Bread, 39
Root Veggie Gumbo, 148–149
Spicy Bean Burgers, 81
Sunset Stew, 147

T

tahini
Baba Ghanoush Soup, 146
Chaat Masala Chickpea Pockets, 63
Fudgy Sesame Chocolate
Mug Cake, 172
Olive Fennel Hummus, 108
Pulled Jackfruit Sandwiches, 71
Sunset Stew, 147
tamari
Fennel Kimchi, 117
Finishing Brown Sauce, 136
Kimchi Fried "Noodz," 88
Mamou's Favorite Miso Bowls, 68–69
Moroccan Quinoa Veggie Bowl, 73–74
Pineapple Fried Rice, 93
Pulled Jackfruit Sandwiches, 71
Red Curry Peanut Sauce, 113
Sichuan-Flavored Mushrooms with
Roasted Shishito Peppers, 77
Sloppy Bulgogi, 89
Smoky Sausages, 70
Smoky Sriracha Tacos, 90
Spicy Glazed Root Veggies, 124
tamarind paste
Pineapple Tamarind Chutney, 64
Red Curry Peanut Sauce, 113
tea
Chaat Masala Peas and Quinoa
Stew, 62
Creton, 102
Fudgy Sesame Chocolate Mug
Cake, 172
Smoky Carrot Spread, 104
tempeh
Mamou's Favorite Miso Bowls, 68–69
Yuzu Koji Tempeh Sandwiches, 67
tofu: Kimchi Fried "Noodz," 88
tomatoes
Chaat Masala Chickpea Pockets, 63
Mushroom Corn Chip Chili, 150
Pomegranate Ezme, 132
Ropa Vieja Tacos, 99
Tomato Hummus Soup, 154
tomato paste
Pulled Jackfruit Sandwiches, 71
Root Veggie Gumbo, 148–149
Sunset Stew, 147
Tomato Hummus Soup, 154
tomato powder: Tomato Hummus Soup,
154
tools
blender, 23
compost bin, 23
fermentation crock, 22

food processor, 23
fruit brush, 23
kitchen scale, 22
salad spinner, 23
spatulas, 23
vegetable brush, 23
turnips
Everything but the Kitchen Sink Leftover Veggies Stew, 138
Root Veggie Gumbo, 148–149
Spicy Glazed Root Veggies, 124

U

Umami Sofrito
Herby Quinoa Frittata, 66
Mushroom Corn Chip Chili, 150
recipe, 119
Sloppy Bulgogi, 89
Spicy Glazed Root Veggies, 124
Tomato Hummus Soup, 154

V

vegetable broth
Baba Ghanoush Soup, 146
Butternut Squash Lasagna, 96–97
Carrot Top–Pea Soup with Pesto, 153
Cashew Sour Cream and Lasagna
Sauce, 95
A Guide to Veggie Broth, 142–143
Herby Quinoa Frittata, 66
Pistachio Dukkah Whole Cauliflower,
83
Queso'rprise, 118
Roasted Onion Soup, 141
Roasted Potato Beer Salad, 122
Root Veggie Gumbo, 148–149
Savory Sweet Cluck-Free Strips Sand-
wiches, 87
Smoky Carrot Spread, 104
Sunset Stew, 147
Umami Sofrito, 119
vital wheat gluten
Smoky Carrot Meatless Balls, 133
Smoky Sausages, 70

W

waffles
Plain Jane Sourdough Waffles, 40
Savory Pickle Waffles, 129
Soured-Oat Hand Waffles, 34
walnuts
Baba Ghanoush Soup, 146
Beer Nut Granola, 48
Chaat Masala Chickpea Pockets, 63
Muhammara, 94
Pomegranate Ezme, 132
Sheet Pan Apple Crisp, 164
Soured-Oat Hand Waffles, 34
wasabi powder: Pulled Jackfruit
Sandwiches, 71

white chocolate chips: Mandarin-White
Chocolate Scones, 28
white onions
Creton, 102
Ropa Vieja Tacos, 99
Sunset Stew, 147
Worcestershire sauce
Roasted Onion Soup, 141
Root Veggie Gumbo, 148–149
Smoky Sausages, 70
Sriracha Barbecue Sauce, 65

Y

yeast spread
Mushroom Corn Chip Chili, 150
Roasted Onion Soup, 141
Ropa Vieja Tacos, 99
Sichuan-Flavored Mushrooms with
Roasted Shishito Peppers, 77
yellow onions
Chaat Masala Peas and Quinoa Stew,
62
Root Veggie Gumbo, 148–149
Sunset Stew, 147
yellow peas
Chaat Masala Peas and Quinoa Stew,
62
Creton, 102
yogurt
Breakfast Greena Colada, 35
Cashew Sour Cream and Lasagna
Sauce, 95
Chaat Masala Chickpea Pockets, 63
Coconut Carrot Cookies, 29
Herby Quinoa Frittata, 66
Labneh, 127
Lemon Curd Muffins, 42
Moroccan Cranachan, 162
Overnight Granola Bowl, 44
Roasted Potato Beer Salad, 122
Zippy Herb Dressing, 75
yuzu paste: Yuzu Koji Tempeh
Sandwiches, 67

Z

za'atar spice mix
Herby Quinoa Frittata, 66
Labneh, 127
Pomegranate Ezme, 132
Za'atar Chutney, 125
zucchini
Moroccan Quinoa Veggie Bowl, 73–74
My Favorite Bowl of Veggies, 84